Down House: the Home of Charles Darwin

Tori Reeve

Introduction

Above: *Daguerreotype portrait of Charles Darwin and his eldest son, William, in 1842, the year the Darwins moved to Down House. This is the only known photograph of Darwin with a member of his family*

Facing page: *Down House from the garden, with family members on the verandah, 1870s*

Down House is celebrated as the home of the great scientist Charles Darwin (1809–82), who lived here for 40 years, from 1842 until his death. Down was also home to Darwin's wife, Emma, their ten children, a modest number of domestic staff, and an assortment of pets and livestock.

Situated in the rural Kent village of Downe, the house offered all the peace and privacy that Darwin needed to work on his revolutionary scientific theories. It was here that he developed his landmark theory of evolution by natural selection and wrote his groundbreaking work *On the Origin of Species by Means of Natural Selection* (1859).

In the decades after the book's publication, Darwin developed his theory and published several key works based on his observations at Down, among them *The Variation of Animals and Plants Under Domestication* (1868) and *The Descent of Man, and Selection in Relation to Sex* (1871). The extensive grounds were remodelled to create a sheltered garden, and Darwin used them as his open-air laboratory. He cultivated plant specimens in his greenhouse and devised botanical experiments to study plant adaptations, often encouraging his children to assist in collecting evidence to support his theories.

Today, the ground-floor rooms of the house have been recreated to look as they did in Darwin's time, with the aid of photographs taken in the 1870s. Many original artefacts, removed when the Darwin family left the house at the turn of the 19th century, were returned when Down House became a museum in 1929, and the family continues to lend and donate items. Visitors can now experience the house and grounds that Darwin so loved, and follow in the footsteps of one of the greatest scientists and thinkers of modern times.

House Tour

The ground-floor rooms are filled with family portraits, furniture and personal possessions, just as they were when Darwin lived here. From the battered horsehair chair in the Old Study, Darwin would have communicated his ideas to friends and colleagues in the scientific world. Today, his study is still crammed with his scientific instruments, books and papers, and the living rooms crowded with the family's furniture and paintings. Upstairs, the first-floor rooms include an exhibition on Darwin's life and work.

FOLLOWING THE HOUSE TOUR

The tour of the house starts in the shop (originally Darwin's New Study) and finishes in the first-floor exhibition. The small numbered plans in the margins highlight the key points of the tour.

EXTERIOR

Approaching Down House today, it is still possible to discern the plain, square block of the original Georgian building amid the many subsequent additions and alterations. Charles Darwin moved here in the autumn of 1842 with his wife Emma and two young children, Annie and William. 'It is a good, very ugly house, with 18 acres,' Darwin wrote to his friend and cousin William Darwin Fox a few months after their arrival. Over the next 40 years, Darwin doubled the size of the house and made numerous minor alterations and ad hoc improvements, changing the use of rooms as the needs of his work and his growing family and household staff dictated.

1 HALLWAY AND SHOP (NEW STUDY)

The portico doorway is one of the earliest additions that Darwin made to the house and was created by adding a passage along the right-hand side of the building, thereby blocking off the previous north-facing entrance. In 1876, in his final campaign of improvement, Darwin added an extension to provide, as he instructed his architect Mr Marshall, 'a billiard room (25ft & 21ft) with bedroom and drawing room above'. The addition of this two-storey block completed the north wing of Down House as it stands today.

In the last few years of his life Darwin moved his study into the billiard room, now fitted out as the shop and ticket office. This became known as the New Study and, as contemporary photographs show, Darwin favoured a similar room layout to his old study, transferring the corner shelves and pigeonholes to the blind alcove to the right of the chimney breast, and squaring off the room using a long bookcase to match the dimensions of his old study. He also kept the exact, meaningful arrangement of portraits and ephemera above the picture rail and tucked around the mantelpiece.

2 DRAWING ROOM

In 1856 Emma gave birth to their tenth and last child, Charles Waring, an event that seems to have contributed to the bout of building work that began shortly afterwards. Charles and Emma agreed that they had 'quite outgrown' their current suite of rooms, and so Darwin instructed his architect to devise 'a new dining room and large bedroom over it'. When the new ground-floor room was finished, however, the Darwins

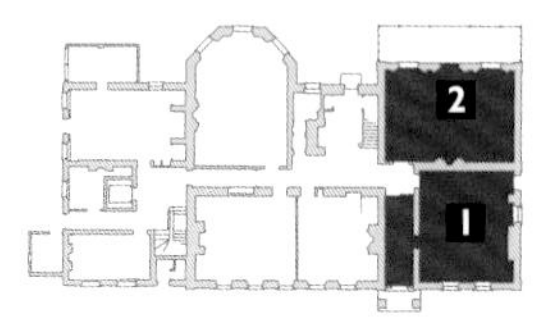

Below: *The New Study in 1880. Darwin worked here for the last few years of his life. He was a man of routine, and the room was arranged in the same way as his old study, even down to the portraits above the mantelpiece*

Facing page: *The front porch, remodelled in 1876 when the new extension was added*

Above: *A pair of chalk and watercolour drawings by George Richmond of Emma and Charles Darwin, 1840*
Right: *'Mr Darwin's drawing room wore a delightfully comfortable and every-day look, with books and pictures in profusion, and a large table in the middle covered with papers, periodicals and literary miscellany.' From* New Monthly Magazine*, 1884*

decided to use it as a drawing room instead. It was generously proportioned and wonderfully light, with floor-to-ceiling windows and French doors opening on to the lawn. Large-paned windows were in fashion following the abolition of the window tax in 1851, and it was at this time that Darwin probably replaced the dining-room bay windows in a similar style.

Emma's initial trip to London to choose wallpaper for the new room was not a success: 'Mama went up yesterday and brought down two such patterns, of the exact colour of mud streaked with rancid oil, that we have all exclaimed against them', Darwin confided to their son William in July 1859. The family chose instead a 'crimson flock-paper with gold stars', typical of the rich palette then in vogue. This was replaced with a more restrained floral pattern when the north wing was expanded and redecorated in 1876. The current scheme is a recreation based on photographs of the drawing room in this later period, using a blue sprigged paper similar to contemporary William Morris designs.

The drawing room was Emma's domain and it was from here that she would have issued instructions to the cook or nursemaid, tended to a fractious child, or cared for the plants in Mrs Maling's patented plant case, a replica of which now stands in front of the French doors. At night, Charles and Emma duelled over their daily game of backgammon, keeping a tally throughout their lifetime that had Charles edging slightly ahead. The centrepiece of the room, then as now, was Emma's treasured Broadwood piano, installed when the room was barely finished in 1858. An accomplished pianist, Emma is said to have taken a few lessons from Chopin when he was staying and teaching in London in the 1840s. After a day in his study, Charles could be found lying on the chaise longue in front of the fire, listening to Emma play. 'She had a crisp and fine touch,' her daughter Henrietta recalled. 'There was always vigour and spirit, but not passion.'

The chaise longue and piano still occupy the same positions, flanked on either side by George Richmond's portraits of the couple, painted in 1840, the year following their marriage: Charles at 31 with his defining heavy brow; Emma pert and brown-eyed, looking younger than her 32 years. It is interesting to compare Emma's likeness in this portrait with the chalk drawing of her by Charles Fairfax Murray, hanging by the door into the inner hallway, sketched many years and many children later.

'We were always free to go where we would & that was chiefly the drawing room and about the garden, so that we were very much with both my Father & Mother', recalled the Darwins' daughter, Henrietta Litchfield

Family Life at Down House

Because of their own liberal upbringing, Charles and Emma were unusually broad-minded Victorian parents. Both had a profound respect for their offspring as individuals, and from a young age their children were encouraged to express themselves freely at work and play. According to Henrietta, her father 'cared for all our pursuits & interests & lived our lives with us in a way that very few Fathers do'. Emma resorted occasionally to a more traditional method of ensuring complicity from her brood, having 'always a good opinion of a little bribery for getting over small childish difficulties'.

For Emma, life must have been an interminable cycle of pregnancy and weaning, with the rest of her time devoted to her husband's needs and ailments. Several of the children were weak at birth and sickly as children, a fact that caused Darwin to fear that his marriage to a first cousin was the cause. Three of the children died young, Mary within weeks of birth, Charles Waring of scarlet fever when it tore through the village in 1858, and the eldest daughter, Annie, at the age of ten from what was probably tuberculosis – a 'bitter & cruel loss' from which Darwin never truly recovered.

The surviving five boys and two girls flourished at Down. They played games in the hall, chased pets around the garden, and wheedled squares of gingerbread from Mrs Evans, the cook. They had each other as playmates, as well as many Wedgwood cousins who came to stay with Uncle Hensleigh or Uncle Jos (Emma's brothers).

Darwin, who had worried that marriage would prevent him his 'choice of Society & little of it', resigned himself with goodwill to the constant supply of Wedgwoods and friends around the dining-room table at lunch.

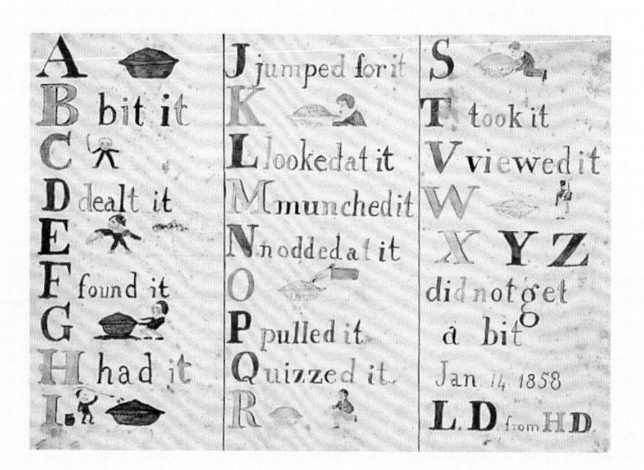

Above: *Emma reading in the dining-room window, with some of her children, 1860s. From left: Leonard, Henrietta (Etty), Horace, Emma, Elizabeth (Bessy), Francis (Frank) and an unknown visitor*

Below: *A watercolour alphabet from Horace Darwin's scrapbook, 1850s*

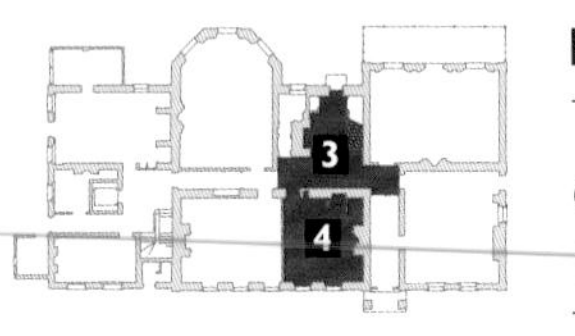

Below right: *The inner hallway in the early 20th century, when Down House was home to Downe House School (see page 51). Darwin stored the first pencil sketch of his species theory, completed in 1842, in the cupboard under the stairs*
Below: *The Darwin children's slide* in situ *on the stairs in the inner hallway*

3 INNER HALLWAY

The present inner hallway is a remodelling of the original 18th-century entrance hall, carried out in 1876 at the time of the north-wing extension. The Darwin children adopted it as their playroom. To assist them in their capers, Darwin had Mr Lewis, a carpenter from the village, construct a long mahogany trough which, when positioned across the run of eight steps beneath the upper-hallway window, transformed the stairway into a slide. Seated on a cushion to aid momentum, the children took turns to propel themselves from the top of the slide, crashing into the wall at the half-landing moments later. The stair-slide that Darwin had made has been returned to Down House by the family and can now be seen on the first floor.

With children careening around the inner hallway in pursuit of one another or Bran, their pet terrier, the hallway was decorated simply for practical reasons. The scheme has been recreated with plain duck-egg blue walls and a linoleum floor robust enough to resist scuffing. The series of chromolithograph prints that adorns the walls, showing religious subjects taken from Old Master paintings, was inherited by Emma on the death of her older sister Charlotte in 1862. The portrait of Darwin by John Collier is a copy made by the artist from the original, painted in 1881 and commissioned by, and still hanging in the apartments of, the Linnean Society at Burlington House in London.

Tucked away by the garden door is a small cupboard, remembered by Gwen Raverat, Darwin's granddaughter, as 'the place of all others where the essence of the whole house was concentrated'. Here, amid cricket bats, croquet mallets and a box of old jottings that the children raided for paper, Darwin kept the 1842 pencil sketch that first outlined his theory of evolution by natural selection and which formed the basis of *On the Origin of Species* 15 years later. This he entrusted to Emma with a letter to be opened 'in the case of my sudden death' instructing her to devote £400 to its publication. 'I have just finished my sketch of my species theory', he wrote. 'If, as I believe that my theory is true & if it be accepted even by one competent judge, it will be a considerable step in science.'

Above: The Old Study, with pigeonhole shelves in the right-hand corner and partitioned 'privy' to the left. Above the fireplace hang Darwin's portraits of Joseph Hooker, Charles Lyell and Josiah Wedgwood I

4 OLD STUDY

One of the things that most attracted Darwin to Down House was the room he described as the 'capital study', which became the centre of his daily routine. At first glance, the room appears unremarkable, square and rather small. Being on the north side of the house, it is disturbed by only an hour or two of direct sunshine in the early morning and, with its tall windows further shielded by wooden shutters, the study provided the perfect cold-light conditions that Darwin found best for undertaking detailed scientific work.

Structurally unaltered since Darwin's day, the study contains almost every piece of original furniture and dozens of his possessions. The room was first restored in 1929 to its appearance in the 1870s, with evidence for its decoration and arrangement based on a detailed contemporary photograph and recollections from Darwin's two surviving sons. The wallpaper and fixtures of the 1929 restoration have also been preserved.

Darwin arranged the furniture for practicality and convenience, centred on the rectangular Pembroke table. This was his principal worktable, usually scattered with scientific instruments, books and correspondence. He sat on the mahogany-framed horsehair armchair at one corner of the table, hunched over a cloth-covered writing board that he balanced across the chair's arms, gradually wearing away the upholstery beneath. To make the chair better suited to his long-legged frame, Darwin had it raised up on cast-iron legs culled from a bed-frame, with a wooden strut nailed roughly across the front to support the backs of his knees.

As with most of the furniture in this room, the chair had castors added to its legs to allow Darwin to move easily about from one workspace to another. To his left was the baize-topped drum table laid with glass-stoppered bottles and insect specimens stored in tiny prescription pillboxes. Darwin rested his feet on a squat maple-wood horsehair stool that he would push to the window and sit on when he needed better light for examining specimens under the microscope.

The alcove shelving to the right of the fireplace is a reconstruction of the original, and is where Darwin kept his books and papers; the pigeonhole shelves were used to file notes of

Key to some of Darwin's possessions on the Pembroke table in the Old Study:

1 Pocketbooks

2 Cloth-covered writing board

3 Letters and postcards

4 Microscope

5 String box

work in progress. The tight arrangement of shelves in this corner is reminiscent of the close quarters of Darwin's cabin space on HMS *Beagle* (recreated on the first floor). By his own admission, years of working in a confined space had forced Darwin to be methodical.

On the south wall, bookcases now house a portion of Darwin's scientific library on loan from the Botany School in Cambridge by arrangement with the University Library. Darwin received parcels of books from his many contacts from across the world. Some remained unread, their pages left uncut, but many were peppered with annotations in Darwin's hand, and, in the case of a few heavy volumes, ripped in half for the sake of convenience.

Shortly after his return in 1836 from the voyage on HMS *Beagle*, Darwin was troubled with stomach problems, which stayed with him for the rest of his life and meant that he suffered frustrating months of inactivity. As a result of this condition, the left-hand corner of the room was partitioned and curtained off as a makeshift privy.

When he was in reasonable health, Darwin worked to a fairly fixed routine. Beginning his day with a short walk before breakfast, he then worked in his study until noon, with a break mid-morning to attend to any domestic affairs with Emma. At midday, he took a longer stroll around the Sandwalk, perhaps in the company of one or more of his children, returning for lunch at about one o'clock. He then read the newspapers, wrote letters and took another walk before returning to his study at 4.30pm. An hour or so later he would rest, before dining early and spending the evening quietly in the drawing room.

On the basis of this routine, Darwin's work continued apace as he pondered the contents of the notebooks brought back from the voyage and developed his thoughts on the transmutation of species. In 1844 he finished a series of three books on the geology of the voyage of HMS *Beagle*, which established his credentials as a geologist. An engraved portrait of his mentor Charles Lyell, president of the Geological Society of London (now the Royal Geological Society), appears above the fireplace, flanked by engravings on the right of Darwin and Emma's grandfather, Josiah Wedgwood I, and on the left an 1868 photograph of the botanist Joseph Dalton Hooker, director of the Royal Botanic Gardens at Kew, by Julia Margaret Cameron. Although Hooker did not agree initially with Darwin's nascent theory of the transmutation of species, the two were close friends. It was Hooker who pushed Darwin to

Facing page: *Darwin's drum table scattered with bottles and pillboxes used for storing insect and seed specimens*

12

Right: Darwin in his Study *by the Russian artist Evstafieff, 1950s, one of two paintings by Evstafieff donated to the museum by the Darwin Museum of Natural History in Moscow*
Below: *A colour plate from Darwin's* Monograph on the Sub-class Cirripedia, *published in 1854 and the culmination of eight years' work*

undertake the reclassification of the entire barnacle sub-class, an endeavour that proved his qualities as a zoologist. Darwin's work on barnacles occupied him for eight years, prompting one of his children to wonder of a friend's father, 'Then where does he do his barnacles?', as though all fathers were similarly employed.

Away from his life as a scientist and the hours spent in his study, Darwin was often interrupted by household events beyond his door. The children remembered being allowed to join their father in the study, 'tucked up on the sofa looking at the old geological map' when unwell. Annie, his eldest daughter, endeared herself by darting into his study with a pinch of snuff (to which Darwin was somewhat addicted) from the jar on the hallway bookcase. His daughter Henrietta recalled years later in private notes for a biography of her father: 'It is proof of how good a playfellow he was, of the kind of terms we were on together, that Leonard when he was about four years old tried to bribe him to come out & play with him during working hours by offering him sixpence.'

5 BILLIARD ROOM

For their first 16 years at Down House the Darwins used this space as a dining room. It became the billiard room in 1858 when the dining room was relocated across the corridor. Darwin's interest in billiards stemmed from the visits he made around this time to Moor Park, a hydropathic resort in Surrey. The new billiard table was bought from the proceeds of the sale of a few Wedgwood reliefs. 'We have set up a billiard table,' Darwin wrote to his cousin William Darwin Fox in March 1859, 'and I find it does me a deal of good and drives the horrid species out of my head.' Whenever he wanted to play he would tug the bell-pull in the Old Study to summon the butler, Parslow, to a game.

In 1876 the room became a study for Darwin's son Francis, who had returned to the family home with his baby son, Bernard, after the death in childbirth of his wife Amy. No photographs exist of the room before this change, and so the billiard room today is based on the evidence of previous paint schemes. The walls are hung with a number of portraits of Darwin: to the right of the fireplace is a photograph of him approaching middle age; to the left are two photographs showing him with the full beard that more commonly defines him. Along the right-hand wall are a number of caricatures of Darwin and other members of his circle, all of which appeared in print after the publication of *On the Origin of Species* in 1859.

6 DINING ROOM

Shortly after the Darwins moved to Down House in 1842, this room was transformed by the addition of a deep, three-storey bay which threw in light and gave views out towards the garden. The windows were originally twelve-pane sashes, like those on the floor above, but in the late 1850s they were enlarged and refitted with two vast panes that could be opened in good weather.

At first this was used as a drawing room, but after the major expansion of 1858 it became the dining room. This was where lunch was served at one o'clock, which was often Darwin's only unavoidable social engagement of the day, especially if numbers were swollen with visiting friends, colleagues and relations. Darwin had a taste for exotic fruit that was occasionally satisfied by his friend Joseph Hooker's sending him bananas cultivated in the hothouses at Kew Gardens.

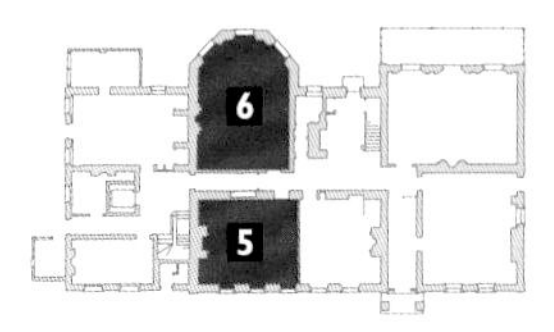

Below: *The billiard room, which was converted from the dining room in 1858. Shortly after the arrival of the billiard table in 1859 Darwin wrote to his son William, 'I have been playing a good deal at Billiards and have lately got up to my play and made some splendid strokes'*

Above: *A compass-clinometer used by Darwin on the* Beagle
Right: The Beagle in the Murray Narrow, Tierra del Fuego *by Conrad Martens*
Below: *Specimen box with beetle fragments pinned to the base, and identifying labels in Darwin's hand*

The Voyage of the *Beagle*, 1831–6

Charles Darwin observed beauty and desolation in equal measure, and 'thrilled with delight' at the wondrous geological formations he saw

Darwin's voyage on HMS *Beagle* was, by his own admission, the most extraordinary period of his life, and one that he said, 'determined my whole career'. He had returned home from Cambridge in August 1831 to find a letter from the botanist and mineralogist John Henslow – who had inspired him in his passion for natural history – suggesting that he might like to put his name forward as gentleman companion to Captain Robert FitzRoy on board HMS *Beagle*. The *Beagle* was due to depart in October, the object of the voyage being, as Darwin explained to his sister Susan, 'to make maps of Eastern side of Tierra del Fuego & Patagonia; likewise to settle Longitude of many places more accurately than they are at present'.

Having secured permission from his father with some difficulty, Darwin bought scientific equipment and firearms. The books he packed for his journey included the recently published first volume of *Principles of Geology* (1830) by Charles Lyell, and a German bible, with which he hoped to improve his German.

HMS *Beagle* finally set sail on 27 December 1831, reaching the Cape Verde Islands in January 1832. Life on board was uncomfortable, and Darwin spent the first months of the voyage largely confined to his cabin because of seasickness. While at sea, he worked at the ship's chart table, which was squeezed into the poop cabin, sharing his quarters by day and sleeping in a hammock slung awkwardly across the tiny space. When the *Beagle* reached land Darwin made long excursions lasting weeks, sometimes months. He filled his satchel with specimens, and made copious notes and sketches in a series of small pocketbooks. In the evenings, he prepared his finds for transport back to Henslow in Cambridge, skinning and cleaning birds and mammals, and packing plants, bones and rock specimens into barrels for shipping. He also wrote letters home and kept a journal detailing his experiences and impressions of what he saw.

Over five years, the *Beagle* sailed to Rio de Janeiro, Montevideo, Tierra del Fuego and Cape Horn, the Falkland Islands, Patagonia, the west coast of South America, the Galapagos Islands, Tahiti and New Zealand. The last leg covered Australia, the Keeling Islands, Mauritius and Cape Town, reaching St Helena and Ascension Island in July 1836. During this time Darwin observed beauty and desolation in equal measure, and 'thrilled with delight' at the geological formations he saw and understood through Lyell's *Principles of Geology*. He even

experienced volcanic eruptions and earthquakes, witnessing the catastrophic effects of the latter at Concepción on the Chilean coast at first hand: 'the most awful yet interesting spectacle I ever beheld'.

During his travels, Darwin endeared himself to his travelling companions, using his hunting skills to join in providing meat for the crew, and handling the temperamental FitzRoy with care. On occasion, he did fall out with his captain, most notably in Brazil, when he found himself nearly ordered off the ship for arguing against slavery.

At the same time, Darwin's experiences and observations were transforming him from a keen amateur into an accomplished naturalist. He made impressive discoveries, unearthing the bones of extinct mammals – such as those of the giant ground sloth Megatherium – some of which were dug out with a hammer and pick-axe from cliffs near Bahia Blanca, about 400 miles south of Buenos Aires. Such finds were later received with great excitement in England. His encounters with the inhabitants of Tierra del Fuego left Darwin amazed at 'the difference between wild and civilized man'. Conrad Martens (1801–78), the ship's artist, depicted the Fuegians hailing the ship in *Beagle in the Murray Narrow, Tierra del Fuego,* a version of which Darwin had framed, and which he later hung in the Old Study at Down House, where it can still be seen today.

Darwin arrived home on 2 October 1836 and began to forge new relationships with colleagues in the scientific world, including Richard Owen, professor of anatomy at the Royal College of Surgeons, and the influential geologist Charles Lyell, then president of the Royal Geological Society. He presented a paper at the Geological Society in January 1837 entitled 'Proofs of recent elevation on the coast of Chile', which impressed Lyell and cemented his reputation as a geologist. Darwin had delivered the specimens he had collected to specialists in the field, and with a grant from the Treasury was later able to arrange for their descriptions to be published with illustrations as *The Zoology of the Voyage of HMS Beagle*. The voyage had helped make his name.

Above: *Lithograph of a Galapagos mockingbird (*Mimus parvulus*), from Darwin's* Zoology of the Voyage of HMS Beagle
Left: *Robert FitzRoy, captain of the* Beagle*, by Francis Lane*
Below: *The diary Darwin kept during the voyage of the* Beagle*. He filled more than 700 pages in five years*

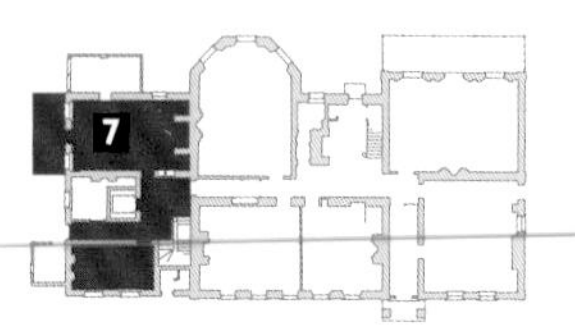

Below: *During the extension works of 1858 the dining room was relocated to what had been the drawing room. It was conservatively decorated and hung with family portraits. The table is set with pieces from the Darwins' Wedgwood 'waterlily' dinner service, originally bought by Darwin's mother. The brown colour scheme was not a commercial success and the pattern was later produced in a more popular blue*

The decoration of the dining room is based closely on a photograph taken in the late 1870s and contemporary wallpaper pattern-books. It suggests that the Darwins chose a conservative scheme as a backdrop to their family portraits, which were recorded in an inventory of the house made in 1882 after Darwin's death. Several of those portraits are found here today, as is the '4ft 6in wide mahogany extending dining table', also mentioned in the inventory, a companion to the mahogany sideboard on loan from the Victoria & Albert Museum. The dinner service on display is part of the Wedgwood 'waterlily' or 'Nelumbium' service that Darwin inherited from his mother, Susannah, who herself had bought it from her brother, Josiah Wedgwood II. It remains here on loan from the Darwin Heirlooms Trust.

7 KITCHEN, SERVICE WING AND SERVICE YARD

At the south end of the corridor the linoleum terminates, opening on to the stone-flagged lobby of the service wing, created as part of the first major extension of the house in 1846. In need of more bedrooms and a schoolroom for the children, Darwin commissioned the architect Edward Cresy to devise a plan that incorporated a suite of servants' rooms on the ground floor and a service stair to the upper floors. The work was estimated at £300 but, as Darwin explained in a letter to his sister Susan in Shrewsbury: 'It seemed so selfish to make the house so luxurious for ourselves and not comfortable for our servants … so I hope the Shrewsbury enclave will not condemn me for extreme extravagance'.

The Darwins enjoyed good relations with their staff, many of whom stayed for decades. Parslow, the butler, who joined the Darwins in 1839 when they had just married and were living in London, was described by Hooker as 'an integral part of the family'. He remained in service until 1876, resisting all attempts to make him cut his lank hair.

Parslow's pantry leads off the service-wing lobby to the left, while on the right a door leads into the kitchen. Here Mrs Davies the cook had to tolerate Darwin and Parslow boiling up foul-smelling pigeons and rabbits in her kitchen for their skeletons. From 1865, Mary Evans was cook. According to the family, she lacked culinary flair: 'He often said the meat of the dinner was very dull, and the sweets the only part worth,' Darwin's son Francis recalled in later years.

Both the kitchen and pantry are now used as visitor tea rooms but with much of the original panelling and fitted cupboards intact. The door from the kitchen leads on to a service yard (now a tea terrace) where, in 1849, Darwin erected a waist-height tub within a specially constructed

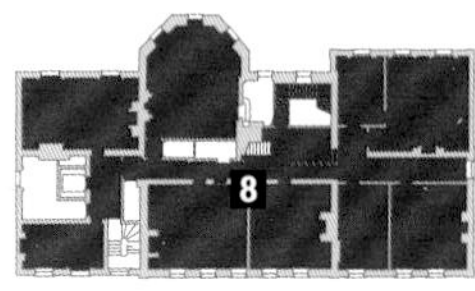

Left: *The Down House staff with Darwin's grandson Bernard on a pony*

wooden shelter near the well, the latter now capped and hidden by bushes. Here, in pursuit of a cure for his persistent stomach problems, he showered with ice-cold water from the cistern above, and was then scrubbed from head to foot by the faithful Parslow. Darwin began his daily 'Diary of Health' at this time to monitor his progress with the water treatment; it is now displayed on the first floor.

8 FIRST-FLOOR ROOMS

At the top of the main staircase hangs a rare oil painting, *Still Life with Insects on Foxgloves*, by Welsh artist Trajan Hughes, inherited by Darwin from his father, Dr Robert Darwin. Just above it, on the sill beneath the upper hallway window, stands a terracotta portrait bust of Darwin's grandfather, Erasmus, by the sculptor William Coffee, dated 1807, on loan from the Darwin Heirlooms Trust.

The main first-floor landing is now a gallery for many of the Darwins' watercolours, notably a pair by the artist Albert Goodwin, capturing the gardens in summer 1880. Also on display are a number of framed photographs, including Leonard Darwin's picture of the Old Study in his father's day, and one of Darwin seated on his horse Tommy outside the front door of Down House (see page 45). Darwin's joyful inscription underneath this latter picture reads, 'Hurrah, no letters today!', indicating how burdensome his correspondence had become by the time the photograph was taken in 1867.

The largest first-floor room, directly above the dining room, was Charles and Emma Darwin's bedroom. It was initially occupied by Emma, who weaned seven of her ten children here, the last of whom was born in 1856 but died two years later. From 1858 Emma and Charles shared the room, at which point it was redecorated. Charles kept his clothes in the adjoining dressing closet.

Using a combination of paint analysis, letters and archival information, the bedroom has been recreated to give an impression of how it might have looked after its redecoration in 1858. The presence of non-scientific books, family photographs and engravings reveals a very personal side to the couple. Charles liked to lie on the sofa and smoke a cigarette while listening to Emma read aloud. He rarely divorced work from leisure, however, and was able to keep an eye on his experiments in the gardens from the large bay window.

The other first-floor rooms now house an exhibition about Darwin's life and work, but in his day they were bedrooms and studies. At the south end of the corridor above the domestic offices was the schoolroom or nursery: a cupboard shelf there still bears a teenage inscription 'W. Darwin 1853'. The view from the right-hand window out towards the mulberry tree was remembered fondly by Darwin's children and grandchildren.

Garden Tour

The garden at Down was central to Darwin's life and work. Here he conducted numerous investigations in the extensive grounds, often enlisting the help of his children. During his daily walks round the shady Sandwalk, Darwin would ponder his day's work, and it was in the hothouse that he made some of his most brilliant discoveries, which resulted in several important botanical works published in the last two decades of his life.

'I write now because the new hot-house is ready, and I long to stock it, just like a schoolboy. Could you tell me pretty soon what plants you can give me; and then I shall know what to order?'
Charles Darwin to Joseph Hooker at Kew Gardens, 1863

FOLLOWING THE GARDEN TOUR

This tour takes the visitor from the lawn and flowerbeds, through the kitchen garden, greenhouses and orchard, to the meadow and Sandwalk beyond. The small numbers correspond to those on the site guide inside the front cover.

Left: Down House from the rear with flowerbeds in full bloom, recreated today as they were in Darwin's time

Facing page: The greenhouses, where Darwin carried out many of his experiments and observations

INTRODUCTION

Darwin bought Down House with 18 acres, which included a lawn, kitchen garden and hay meadow. He added banks and shrubberies for shelter from the cold north wind and Emma chose the flowers to grow in the six formal flowerbeds to one side of the lawn at the back of the house. More fruit trees were planted to provide a plentiful supply of produce.

'The early memories that come back to me', recalled Darwin's daughter, Henrietta Litchfield, in her notes for a biography, 'seem now to be full of sunshine and happiness ... the lawn burnt brown, the gardens a blaze of colour, the six oblong beds in front of the drawing-room windows, phloxes, lilies, and larkspur in the middle and portulacas, gazanias and other low-growing plants in front looking brighter than flowers ever do now.'

The children enjoyed games of croquet and tennis on the lawn, and ran through the knee-deep grasses in the adjoining fields. At the far end of the kitchen garden a sandy, tree-lined path was formed along the south-west perimeter of the estate. The family called it the Sandwalk and Darwin would walk around it every day. Since the 1930s it has also been known as his 'thinking path'. Darwin used his garden as an open-air laboratory in the series of important experiments for *On the Origin of Species,* and his subsequent lines of enquiry led him to build a hothouse for tropical plants in the early 1860s.

9 LAWN AND FLOWERBEDS

The architectural development of Down House is best followed from the lawn at the back of the house. From here, the original square block of the Georgian building is visible behind the three-storey bay that Darwin added in 1843 to give views across the garden in three directions. In 2006 the exterior of the house, painted white for much of the 20th century, was returned to the original colour scheme identified in Albert Goodwin's contemporary watercolours: butterscotch walls with sashes picked out in terracotta and a grey-blue trellis. The trellis runs the full height of the bay and is covered in a blanket of climbing plants in the summer months.

Protruding to the left is the two-storey extension of 1858 that provided a drawing room and extra bedrooms above. Tucked away to the right is the extension added in 1846 to provide domestic offices and a schoolroom on the first floor. This wing is slightly obscured by the mulberry tree that survives from Darwin's day

Right: *Watercolour showing the garden at Down House in the height of summer, by Albert Goodwin, 1880*
Below: *Darwin's granddaughter Gwen Raverat sketched the mulberry tree in the garden for her memoir* Period Piece: A Cambridge Childhood *(1952). The faces of Gwen and her little sister Margaret, daughters of George Darwin, can be seen looking out of the schoolroom window*

with a permanent iron prop to support its weight. In her memoir *Period Piece: A Cambridge Childhood*, Gwen Raverat recalled the giant mulberry tree rising up outside the windows of the schoolroom: 'The shadows of the leaves used to shift about on the white floor, and you could hear the plop of the ripe mulberries as they fell to the ground.' More than a century later the mulberry tree still produces a crop of juicy berries each summer to stain the broad walk that traverses the back of the house from the tea terrace.

The Darwins employed three gardeners to maintain the lawns, the orchard and the kitchen garden. William Brooks and Joseph Comfort both tended the animals on the estate in addition to their gardening duties, and Henry Lettington occasionally helped Darwin with his experiments.

LAWN PLOT AND WORMSTONE EXPERIMENTS

For Darwin, the lawn was not just a place to sprawl beneath 'the row of lime trees humming with bees'. In 1855 he had been surveying the variety of vegetation in Great Pucklands Meadow and he carried out an experiment on his lawn the following year. He marked up a rectangle of mown lawn measuring 4ft by 3ft (122cm by 91cm), and recorded the number of plant species that sprang up within the plot during the course of the year. In the first year Darwin identified 20 different species and, continuing the survey for the next two years, noted that by 1858 only 11 species survived, mostly the coarser and more robust plants and grasses. These experiments demonstrate the simplicity of Darwin's approach to botanical investigation and the clarity of the end results, here revealing biodiversity and supporting his theory of 'survival of the fittest' in the plant world.

Another simple experiment that took place in the north-west corner of the lawn utilized a circular stone slab, which was laid onto the soil with two vertical metal rods bedded in the chalk beneath and protruding up through a hole in the centre of the stone. Darwin's son Horace developed the so-called 'Wormstone' experiment as a way of measuring the movement of soil displaced by the action of worms undermining the stone. With guidance from his father, and the use of a specially designed measuring device, Horace eventually deduced that the stone sank two millimetres a year. Francis Darwin described the experiment in a footnote to a later edition of Darwin's last work *The Formation of Vegetable Mould through the Action of Worms* (1881) and Horace finally published the results of the experiment in a paper in 1896. The wormstone is still bedded in the soil beneath a Spanish chestnut tree, and the measuring device is on display on the first floor.

Left: *Cowslips in full bloom in the kitchen garden*
Below: *Photograph from the late 1850s by William Darwin showing the Darwins' gardeners William Brooks and Henry Lettington on the back lawn with their donkey-drawn mowing machine*

10 KITCHEN GARDEN

The kitchen garden is walled on three sides, with hedging on the south for shelter. A wide range of vegetables is grown there today, from peas and runner beans to turnips, onions, and rhubarb at the far end. Many of the vegetables now grown there are Victorian varieties, specifically noted by Darwin.

In the late 1850s, while writing *On the Origin of Species*, Darwin took over a corner of the kitchen garden for his 'experimental beds'. He had been troubled by recent scientific reports suggesting that primrose seeds (*Primula vulgaris*) could spontaneously produce cowslip (*Primula veris*), a leap that went against his theory of variation produced through the gradual accumulation of small variations through natural selection. In 1859 Darwin planted his experiment bed with both *Primula* species, and the following year noted with satisfaction that primroses only produced primroses and cowslips only produced cowslips.

Far more intriguing to Darwin, however, was his discovery of two different arrangements of the reproductive components of the cowslips, divided equally among the 522 flower stalks that were gathered; while half of the plants had a short style and long stamens, the other half contained a long style and short stamens. Further investigation led him to discover that two distinct forms of the same genus existed in order to compel the insect pollinator to cross-fertilize between the two. Darwin's discovery of 'heterostylous' species was a significant step in his investigations into plant evolution, and in later years formed the basis of *Different Forms of Flowers on Plants of the Same Species* (1877).

Darwin and His Greenhouse

***Orchids:** The greenhouse is stocked with orchids that Darwin grew in order to explore the previously unknown link between insects and orchid pollination*

***Insectivorous plants:** Darwin was fascinated by the form and feeding habits of the sundew* Drosera rotundifolia *with its sticky tentacles that curl in to trap insect prey*

Comet orchid (Angraecum sesquipedale)*: Darwin correctly predicted that one day a moth would be found with a 30cm tongue, capable of reaching this orchid's nectar*

***Climbing plants:** Darwin observed the wild cucumber* Echinocystis lobata *to investigate how climbing plants use their stems and tendrils to find support*

Common toadflax (Linaria vulgaris)*: Through his experiments with common toadflax, Darwin was able to prove the advantages of cross-pollination in plants*

***Above:** Photograph from the 1850s by William Darwin of Henry Lettington, the under-gardener to Brooks who sometimes helped Darwin with his experiments in the garden. Lettington became head gardener in 1872 when Brooks retired*
***Left:** As in Darwin's day, the greenhouse benches are filled with orchids and insectivorous and climbing plants*

III GREENHOUSES

Darwin had first tried to rear tropical plant specimens in the plant case that was bought for the drawing room, but it was too small and the more exotic specimens failed. So, in the early 1860s, he erected a hothouse alongside the greenhouse in the kitchen garden to provide him with the specialized growing environment he needed for experimentation. The compartments adjoined one another, with interconnecting doors and wooden benches on either side running the length of them. Sloping glass roofs captured the sun's rays and a boiler system kept the environment warm and well suited to delicate specimens. Darwin quickly filled his new hothouse laboratory with specimens from his friend Joseph Hooker at Kew, and was soon in the thrall of his new occupation. 'You cannot imagine what pleasure your plants give me', he wrote to Hooker. 'I go and gloat over them'. Darwin jotted his findings in a hardcover exercise book entitled 'Experiment Book', begun in 1855 and kept until 1867. Several important publications emerged from these greenhouse experiments, centred mostly on the growth patterns and reproductive behaviour of plants.

Visitors today will find the greenhouses stocked with the same plant specimens that Darwin cultivated for his botanical research projects, many of which stemmed from subjects that had first pricked his interest elsewhere. As an undergraduate at Cambridge Darwin had studied the reproductive biology of orchids, and was fascinated by the unusual anatomy of the plant with its twin bulbous pollen heads. He had collected rare specimens during his voyage on HMS *Beagle* and now, years later, he investigated his theory of orchid reproduction dependent on insect pollinators. Darwin observed several orchid

Right: *An illustration from* The Century Magazine, 1883, *showing Darwin in his greenhouse*
Below right: *An illustration from Darwin's* On the Various Contrivances by which British and Foreign Orchids are Fertilised by Insects *(1862). It shows the action of the pollen mass of* Orchis mascula, *which attaches itself to the end of a pencil when the point is inserted into a flower in imitation of an insect proboscis. Darwin showed how, as the proboscis is withdrawn, the pollen mass droops downwards ready to be deposited on to the sticky stigma of the next flower, thereby achieving cross-pollination*
Below far right: *Many of Darwin's garden experiments are documented in his 'Experiment Book', which covers a period from 1855 to 1867*

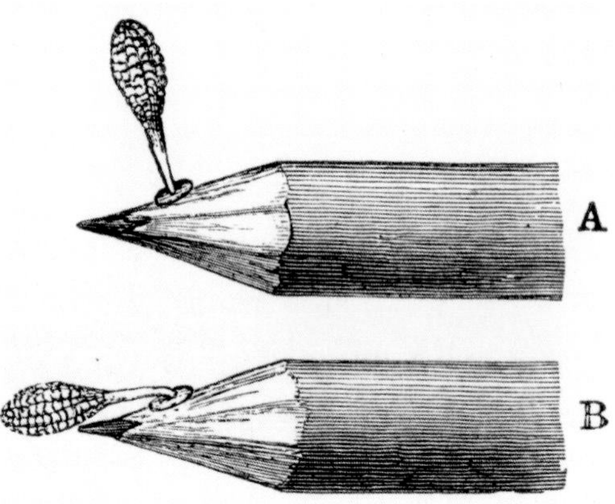

varieties on his greenhouse benches, nurtured exotic deliveries from Hooker, and transplanted specimens spied while walking the Sandwalk or out picnicking with Emma on a nearby spot he called 'Orchis Bank'.

Among his critical findings was the evolution of diverse and beautiful forms of different species of flower to attract specific insect pollinators. The results of his research were published in 1862 in his first purely botanical production, *On the Various Contrivances by which British and Foreign Orchids are Fertilised by Insects*, which was a major contribution to the study of orchid anatomy and plant reproduction.

Darwin's next work, *On the Movements and Habits of Climbing Plants* (1865), developed from his examination of certain climbing-plant species, grown in pots in the greenhouse and winding through the trelliswork fixed to the back of the house. By dedicated observation and copious note-taking Darwin was able to detect what he called circumnutation – the gyrating of the plant stems as they searched for support on their upward climb. Again, Hooker provided Darwin with climbing-plant specimens from the hothouses at Kew. In the mid-1870s Darwin returned to the subject, undertaking research in collaboration with his son, Francis, recently returned to the family home with his infant son after the death of his wife.

The pair observed specimens in the greenhouse, noting their responsiveness to different light conditions and exploring the notion that plants 'sleep' in darkness. The only extant photographs of the inside of the greenhouse date from this time and show examples of the same plant 'awake' and 'asleep', aided by a large sheet pinned up to block out the sun.

Darwin and Francis also installed oat seedlings in a pot on the sill of the Old Study window and noted what Darwin called heliotropism, now called phototropism, where a shaft of light from one direction could override circumnutation (gyration) and instead cause a side-to-side motion. Francis's collaborative effort with his father resulted in *The Power of Movement in Plants* (1880).

Darwin reserved perhaps his greatest fascination for insectivorous plants, in particular the sundew *Drosera rotundifolia*, which he had

first sighted in Sussex in 1860. Alongside his orchids, Darwin cultivated dozens of *Drosera* specimens in terracotta pots on his greenhouse benches. He noted the gradual curling of the *Drosera*'s sticky tentacles around an unsuspecting fly or gnat, and fed them specks of raw meat, egg white and even nail clippings. The illustrations from the resulting work on *Insectivorous Plants* (1875) show the relationship between insect and plant predator, a world apart from the friendly interdependence between the orchid and its insect pollinator. 'At present he is treating *Drosera* just like a living creature', Emma mused at the time, 'and I suppose he hopes to end in proving it to be an animal.'

12 WALLED GARDEN, ORCHARD AND LABORATORY

In 1844 Darwin acquired a plot of land to the west of the house and planted a small orchard, buffered from the winds by a tall flint and red-brick wall lined with flower borders. In 1881 he bought more land to extend the orchard further westward, knocking through an archway into the kitchen-garden wall. In that year a hard tennis court was laid into the lawn at the bottom of the orchard, and a brick darkroom built up against the back wall of the greenhouses.

Darwin died the following year, and there is no evidence that he ever used it. It was later used as a laboratory by pupils at Downe House School. Today the laboratory houses a modern, observational beehive, exploring Darwin's research into the evolutionary development of bee-cell formation. By looking at the nests of bumblebees and the Mexican bee type *Melipona domestica*, Darwin was able to observe distinct evolutionary steps to explain the perfection of hexagonal honeycomb.

As with other areas of the garden, Darwin used the orchard for plant investigation. In January 1857 he began what he called his 'weed garden' experiment in the orchard to examine the survival rate of seedlings when confronted with natural predators. He began by marking off a small section of lawn and removing the turf; he then recorded the number of seedlings that sprang up, marking each with a small length of wire. At regular intervals Darwin monitored the seed survival rate by counting the number of wire markers where the seedling had disappeared. By August Darwin had recorded that, from a total of 357 germinated seedlings, 295 had died 'chiefly by slugs and insects'. As with the 'lawn plot' experiment (see page 20), Darwin was able to show the pressure of natural selection by means of simple, observation-led investigations.

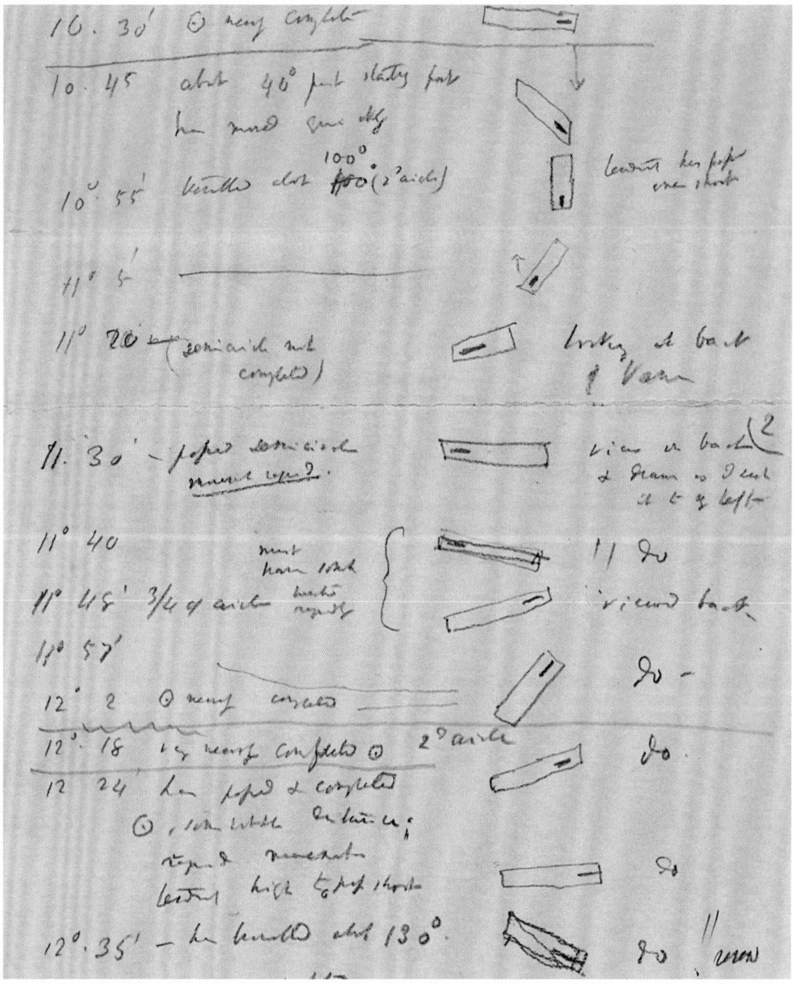

Left: *Pupils at Downe House School in the laboratory at Down House, photographed in the early 20th century*

Below: *Darwin's observations on the gyrating movement of the wild cucumber,* Echinocystis lobata, *the tendrils of which rotate on their journey upwards in search of a solid object. 'Immediately that the tendril touches any object, its sensitiveness causes it immediately to seize it', he wrote*

Above: *View from the Sandwalk looking north towards Great House Meadow*

13 GREAT HOUSE MEADOW

The Darwins also owned Great House Meadow, named after the 17th-century 'Great House' that once stood on the site. The meadow is a 15-acre field of roughly triangular proportions bordering the kitchen garden to the right and stretching across to Luxted Road on the left. It is dotted with beech trees and hawthorns, together with a few specimens of walnut and cherry trees.

Darwin improved the quality of the soil in Great House Meadow by adding layers of coal cinders to it and cutting it for hay. It was also used for grazing the family's two cows, two horses and donkey, but Darwin often monitored its plant and insect activity. It was here in 1854 that he first orchestrated his children to watch for bumblebees buzzing from tree to tree and along the hedgerow, and also established that red clover depends on bumblebees to fertilize its flowers.

Darwin allowed the villagers to use the field for their cricket matches, and in the 1930s, land in the south-east corner was hedged off to make a cricket field with pavilion for Downe Cricket Club. In 2007 English Heritage rebuilt the pavilion to the model of the original, to preserve the long association between Down House and the club.

14 SANDWALK

In 1846 Darwin rented a narrow strip of land at the far end of Great House Meadow from local landowner Sir John Lubbock. He planted a hedge round the plot, with trees and bushes along its border and extended a copse of trees to the south with alder, birch and hornbeam. He also laid down the 'Sandwalk', a stone and sand path beginning at the gate at the bottom of the kitchen garden. The walk passes between Great House Meadow and Great Pucklands Meadow, then runs around the copse, looping back on itself to join up at the midway point. At the furthest point is a sheltered wooden seat where the Darwins' summer house once stood. As a little girl, Darwin's granddaughter Gwen remembered the Sandwalk as 'ominous and solitary', and the Sandwalk copse as 'truly terrifying'. Today, the copse has been thickened by years of growth and from the open pathway flanked by meadows the visitor is plunged into the shadow of large trees.

The Sandwalk was Darwin's 'thinking path', a quarter-mile walk that formed the basis of his daily perambulations around the estate. He made regular circuits, for example, five times round it at noon. The children skipped alongside from time to time, teasing their father by adding stones to the pile he would kick away to count out each lap, but mostly Darwin walked alone, 'using a walking-stick heavily shod with iron which he struck loudly against the ground', as Francis recalled.

The hedgerows and undergrowth of the Sandwalk offered plenty of scope for plant-life investigations. In one place where a small patch of soil had been cleared, Darwin noticed charlock springing up, although it had not grown there, or anywhere else in the plot, for some years. He dug some trial patches and watched as charlock again sprang up, leading him to write a paper entitled *Vitality of Seeds* in which he suggested that 'the power in seeds of retaining their vitality when buried in damp soil may well be an element in preserving the species'.

The Darwins and Village Life

Darwin found Downe 'the quietest country I have ever lived in ... to the east and west there are impassable valleys, to the south only one very narrow lane, and to the north through the village only two other lanes'. The approach to Downe remains little changed, with rough hedgerows, blackberry bushes and a great variety of trees that arch across and knit together in the height of summer growth.

Although the village became Downe with an 'e' in the 1850s to distinguish itself from County Down in Ireland, the Darwins retained the original spelling of 'Down' for their house. In Darwin's day the village consisted of 40 or so houses scattered around the 14th-century flint church of St Mary, and the George and Dragon Inn. A butcher and baker provided basic provisions, and a carrier made a weekly trip to London for special orders. A few larger houses stood within modest plots of land, but most dwellings were cottages, inhabited by tenant farmers and labourers.

The principal landowner of the parish was Sir John Lubbock, a mathematician, astronomer and banker, who lived at High Elms to the north. The Darwin children often played with Sir John's, who were of a similar age. Sir John's eldest boy, John, became a frequent visitor to Down House for informal lessons in natural history and walks with Darwin, and became a respected naturalist. In Darwin, he found a warmth lacking in his austere father.

It was Sir John who put Darwin up for local magistrate duties, a role Darwin took on in 1857 and held for many years. Here, he surprised himself with his severity in comparison to his fellow magistrates, particularly in cases of animal neglect. Etty recalled that her father's 'hatred of oppression or cruelty were very strong as anyone who had ever heard him speak of slavery could testify'.

Darwin became a founding member and treasurer of the Downe Friendly Society, which collected contributions from the villagers for a fund that paid out in case of sickness or death, and also served as treasurer of the Coal Club. The villagers viewed him with 'friendly recognition' and would touch their cap to him as he passed by on his way to the railway station.

Emma was a benevolent force in the village, running a Sunday school and bringing food and medicines to needy households. Often accompanied by Annie and Etty, she would dole out bread and home-made gin cordial, a heady concoction of wine laced with laudanum, sugar, peppermint and bitters.

'My life goes on like clockwork and I am fixed in the spot where I shall end it'
Charles Darwin to Robert FitzRoy

Left: *The village of Downe with the spire of St Mary's visible at the end of the high street*

History

Down House was a place of happy refuge for the Darwin family. The rooms contained a comfortable clutter of furniture, and the carpets were patched when the children wore them threadbare. 'Life was wonderfully simple in those days', recalled Darwin's daughter Henrietta. 'I can see now the patched look of a certain green-flowered carpet in the drawing room, skilfully contrived by my Mother'

Above: *The Mount in Shrewsbury, Darwin's childhood home*
Left: *Charles Darwin and his younger sister, Emily Catherine (Catty), in one of a series of four chalk portraits of the Darwin family on display in the drawing room. The young Darwin cradles a potted plant, hinting at an early interest in natural history*

Facing page: *Colour lithograph of Charles Darwin, one of a series of cartoons depicting 'Men of the Day', from* Vanity Fair, *1871*

DARWIN'S CHILDHOOD

Charles Darwin was born in 1809, to Dr Robert Darwin and his wife, Susannah Wedgwood. The second youngest of six children, Darwin was cared for by his three elder sisters, Marianne, Caroline and Susan, after their mother died in 1817, but he was particularly close to his elder brother, Erasmus, and to his little sister, Emily Catherine, or 'Eras' and 'Catty' as they were known. At the age of nine, Darwin attended Shrewsbury School, as had his brother before him, but he did not take to the classical education he received there and preferred to collect beetles in the woods. He was nicknamed 'Gas' by his classmates for his fondness of devising chemical experiments in an outhouse at home, but at the age of 15 he acquired a new interest, developing a 'zeal for the most holy cause' of shooting. 'You care for nothing but shooting, dogs and rat-catching', Dr Darwin had berated him, 'and you will be a disgrace to yourself and all your family'.

CAMBRIDGE AND ITS AFTERMATH

Like his brother, Darwin was sent to Edinburgh to study medicine, but he quickly realized his incompatibility with the subject and, in 1827, abandoned his degree and returned home.
Dr Darwin then sent his son to Christ's College,

Right: *Ink sketch of Darwin riding a giant beetle and holding aloft an insect net as he pursued his favourite pastime while at Cambridge, by his fellow undergraduate and beetling companion Albert Way*

Below: *Maer Hall, the Wedgwoods' Staffordshire home, possibly drawn by one of the Wedgwood children*

Cambridge, where he enrolled for an ordinary degree in preparation for taking holy orders. At Cambridge, Darwin and his cousin William Darwin Fox went 'beetling' in the nearby fens, and Darwin formed a life-changing friendship with the Revd John Stevens Henslow, a young professor of botany. Although Darwin continued with his studies, he attended Henslow's lectures on plant biology and accompanied him on field trips.

Darwin graduated with a commendable degree in 1831 and began to plan an expedition to Tenerife. In August, however, he received a letter from Henslow with news of a remarkable opportunity: a position had arisen to join the crew of the surveying ship HMS *Beagle* as gentleman companion and naturalist to Captain Robert FitzRoy. Henslow had suggested Darwin for the role 'not on the supposition of yr. being a finished Naturalist, but as amply qualified for collecting, observing, & noting any thing worthy to be noted in Natural History'. Darwin was keen but his father was only prepared to give his consent 'if you can find any man of common sense who advises you to go'. Luckily for Darwin, his uncle Josiah Wedgwood II commended the idea and so Dr Darwin gave his reluctant blessing. The five years spent on board the *Beagle* (see pages 14–15) transformed Darwin from fledgling naturalist to knowledgeable expert and gave him a focus for the rest of his life.

When he arrived home in October 1836, Darwin began to establish his reputation in the scientific world, becoming acquainted with such eminent men as the anatomist Richard Owen and the geologist Charles Lyell, and reading a paper based on his recent travels at the Geological Society. He went on to arrange for publication of *The Zoology of the Voyage of HMS Beagle* in 19 parts, which described the specimens he had collected on his voyage; the work was issued in five volumes between 1839 and 1843.

At his London lodgings in Great Marlborough Street, Darwin pored over his field notebooks, re-examining specimens and wondering about the possibility that species might change as time progressed. In 1837 he began a series of notebooks full of astonishing new ideas about the transmutation of species. On one page he sketched a branching diagram to show the diversification of species from a common ancestor (see page 41). This famous diagram represents Darwin's first attempt to describe his theory of evolution.

__Left:__ Pencil drawing by George Scharf showing Upper Gower Street in 1840, at a time when Darwin and Emma were living here

TO MARRY OR NOT TO MARRY

In 1838, as he worked through his thoughts on transmutation, Darwin began to contemplate another big question: marriage. This may have been due to a recent encounter with his cousin Emma Wedgwood, whom he had known since childhood and who had, since his return, marked herself out as a lively and intelligent presence at Maer Hall, the Staffordshire home of the Wedgwoods. For Darwin, however, the notion of marriage was bound up with fear of a life given up to social and parental duties, with no time for scientific work. True to his analytical nature, Darwin weighed up the merits of marriage in a list scribbled under two headings 'Marry' and 'Not Marry'. The results were in favour of matrimony.

For her part, Emma had been hoping that 'he would really like me' if he saw more of her, and when the proposal came at Maer Hall on 11 November 1838, she accepted immediately. Both the Darwin and Wedgwood families were delighted, and Emma gave free rein to her feelings for her fiancé: 'He is the most transparent man I ever saw and every word expresses his real thoughts', she wrote to her Aunt Jessie soon after the proposal. A few days before their marriage on 29 January 1839, Darwin wrote to Emma: 'I think you will humanize me, & soon teach me there is greater happiness, than building theories, & accumulating facts in silence and solitude.'

MARRIED LIFE

Darwin and Emma moved into a tall, thin terraced house on Upper Gower Street in London, a short walk from the British Museum. They immediately went 'sloping through the snow to Broadwood's' to buy a piano for the first-floor drawing room. 'It makes the room look so much more comfortable', Emma noted; 'I have given Charles a large dose of music every evening'. Ranged over three floors, the rooms may have been comfortable but they were unattractive. Etty described how her father laughed at the ugly furnishings, which 'combined all the colours of a macaw in hideous discord', an observation that led to the house being known as Macaw Cottage.

At the end of 1839 Emma gave birth to their first child, William Erasmus. 'What an awful affair a confinement is', Darwin wrote to his cousin William Darwin Fox after the birth; 'it knocked me up almost as much as it did Emma'. Even so, within months Emma was pregnant again, this time

Facing page: *A watercolour of the Darwin children's Wedgwood cousins, now on display in the drawing room. Sophy, Margaret and Lucy Wedgwood were the daughters of Emma's brother Josiah III, and Charles's sister Caroline*

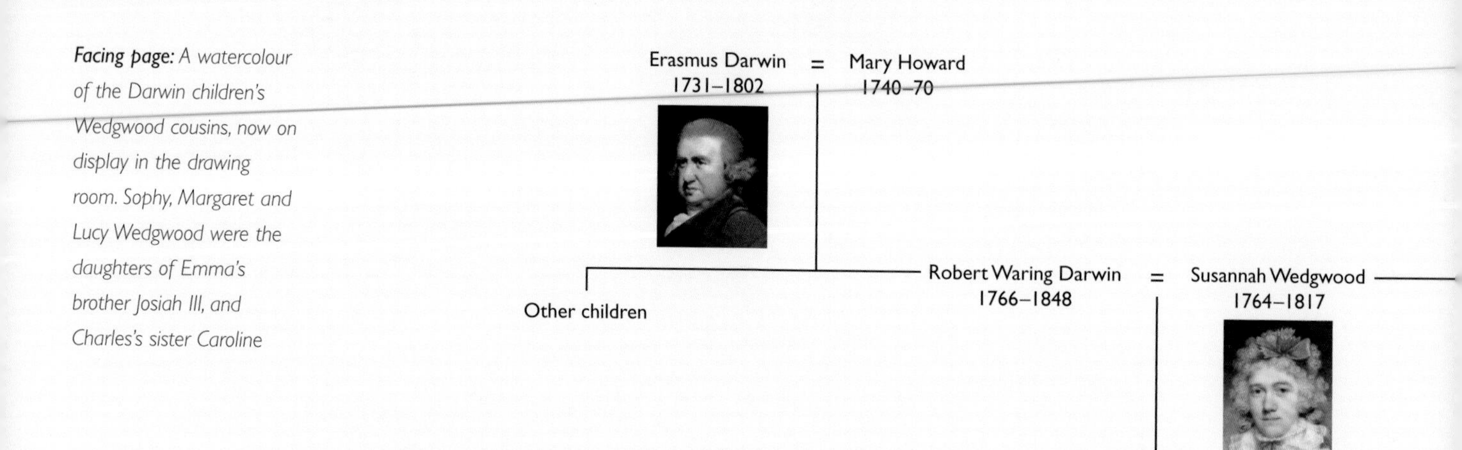

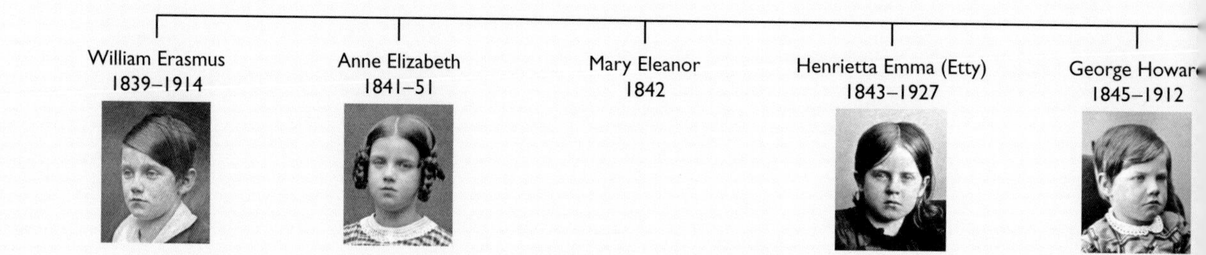

The Wedgwood and Darwin Families

Charles Darwin and his wife, Emma Wedgwood, were first cousins. Their family relationships were founded, in the later 18th century, upon the friendship between two members of prominent Midlands families – the physician and natural philosopher Erasmus Darwin and the potter Josiah Wedgwood I. Both men were 'Lunaticks', members of an assembly of like-minded scientists, philosophers and physicians known as the Lunar Society, the intellectual prowess of which was instrumental in steering the technological advances of the Industrial Revolution.

When one of Erasmus's sons, Robert, married Josiah I's daughter Susannah, the alliance wove the families closer together and brought the Darwin and Wedgwood cousins into frequent company.

Robert Darwin marshalled his household at The Mount in Shrewsbury with stern authority. Large, overbearing and temperamental, he became more so after the death of his wife in 1817, when Charles was only eight years old. As a teenager, Charles's obvious preference for sport over his work at Shrewsbury School angered his father, who predicted that Charles would become a disgrace to himself and to his family. Understandably, it mattered to Darwin that his father thought well of him: 'I think my Father was a little unjust to me when I was young', he recollected later in life, 'but afterwards I am thankful to think I became a prime favourite with him.'

Just over the border in Staffordshire, on the other hand, life at Maer Hall, Emma Wedgwood's family home, brought nothing but joy to the visiting Darwins. According to Etty, Maer was the place Darwin 'always talked of with intense enjoyment'. In 1837 another marriage entwined the families further when Charles's older sister Caroline married Josiah

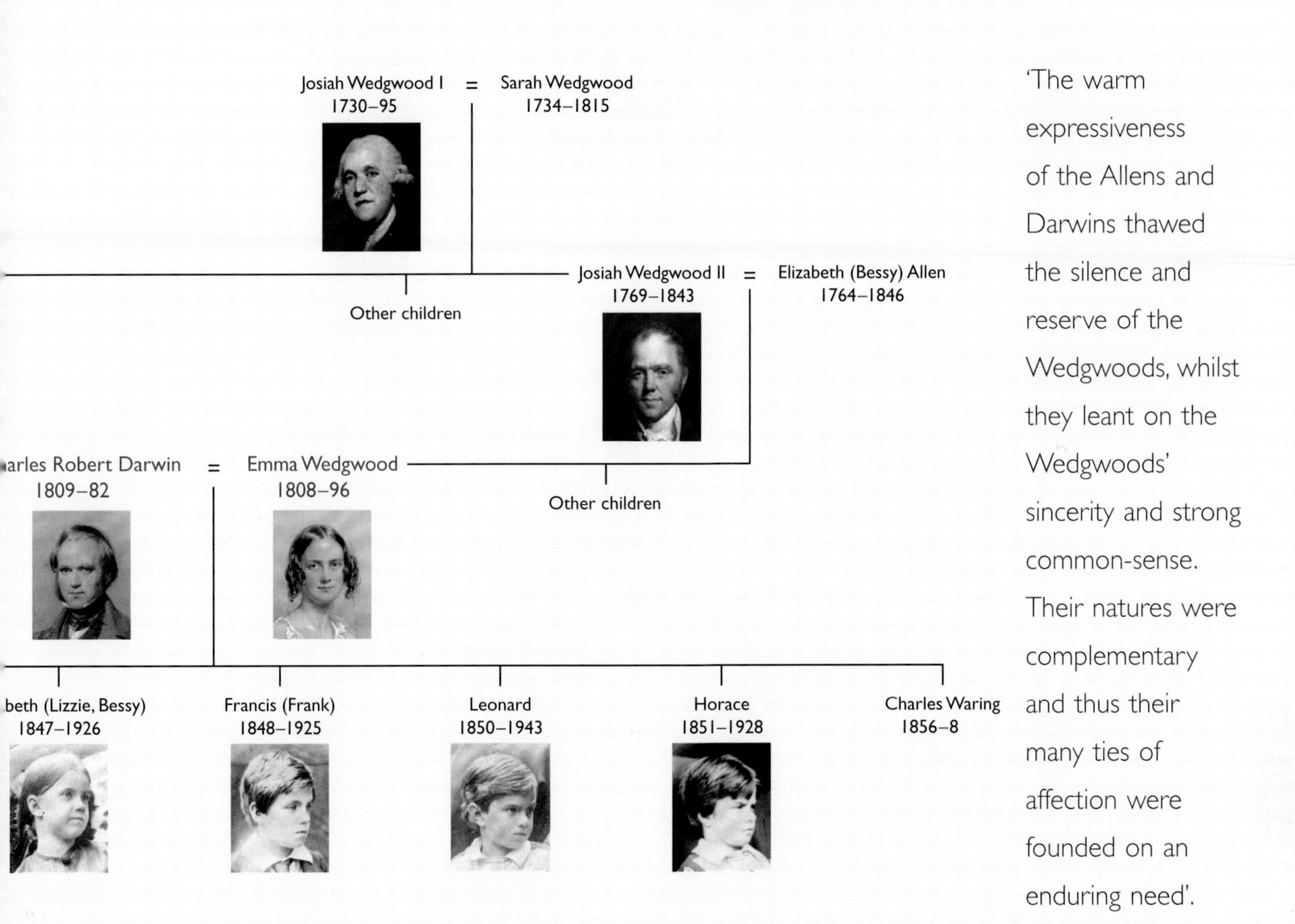

'The warm expressiveness of the Allens and Darwins thawed the silence and reserve of the Wedgwoods, whilst they leant on the Wedgwoods' sincerity and strong common-sense. Their natures were complementary and thus their many ties of affection were founded on an enduring need'.

From Henrietta Litchfield's notes for a biography

Wedgwood III. Members of both families now cast their eyes optimistically towards Emma and Charles, the latter recently returned from his voyage on the *Beagle*. When Darwin proposed on 11 November 1838, it was the cause of much rejoicing, as borne out by a letter Darwin wrote to Emma around this time: 'My father echoes and re-echoes uncle Jos's words, "You have drawn a prize!" Certainly no man could by possibility receive a more cordial welcome than I did from every one at Maer … My life has been very happy and very fortunate, and many of my pleasantest remembrances are mingled up with scenes at Maer, and now it is crowned. My own dear Emma, I kiss the hands with all humbleness and gratitude, which have so filled up for me the cup of happiness – it is my most earnest wish I may make myself worthy of you.'

Above: *Emma Darwin with four-year-old Leonard in 1854. At the time this photograph was taken Emma was 46 and had given birth to nine children. Her tenth and final child, Charles Waring, would follow in 1856*
Below: *A watercolour of Down House from the garden by one of the children*

Facing page: *The Sandwalk photographed by Leonard Darwin in the 1870s. The path ahead leads back to the kitchen garden*

carrying the additional burden of a sick husband. While visiting Maer, Darwin had suffered his first attack of illness since his return from the *Beagle* voyage. He was laid low with stomach pains and skin rashes that made concentrating on scientific work impossible, and back at Gower Street he spent hours in the nursery playing with baby William. In William, nicknamed 'Doddy', Darwin found a new and fascinating subject for his keen mind and noted that he had discovered 'a fine degree of paternal fervour'.

In March 1841 Emma gave birth to a second child, Anne Elizabeth, known as Annie. The need for more space, and a desire to escape the interminable round of social engagements that London brought, prompted the Darwins to search for a new home in the country.

THE MOVE TO DOWN

Although 'old and ugly', Down House was precisely what the Darwins were looking for: a house 'at the extreme verge of the world' with room for expansion, acres of land, and neighbours who were neither 'too near nor too far', as Emma noted with approval. The primary motivation for moving to the countryside was for the benefit of the children. In the summer of 1842 Emma was six months pregnant with her third child, and liberation from their cramped London quarters on Gower Street became all the more pressing. The couple and their young family moved into Down on 24 September 1842. Life in the new house began in the shadow of the death at three weeks of the new baby, Mary Eleanor, but with characteristic stoicism Charles and Emma threw themselves into exploring their new surroundings, with 'dear little things' Willy and Annie.

LIFE AT DOWN

Darwin wasted little time in putting his plans for improving Down House into operation. The following spring he oversaw, among other works, the addition of a full-height bay with views across the garden that did much to soften the façade. He also had the lane at the front of the house diverted and dug down a few feet to give the family more privacy from the 'intolerable' gaze of passers-by travelling from Downe village.

A year after the move to Down, Darwin wrote to his cousin William Darwin Fox: 'I have now got this place in order ... & I think when you next see it, you will think it greatly improved'. Having established life at the new house, Darwin was able to enjoy a period of intense concentration on practical scientific work and publication in the next decade.

Darwin completed his trilogy on the geology of South America that he had begun in 1842 with *The Structure and Distribution of Coral Reefs*, publishing *Volcanic Islands* in 1844 and *Geological Observations on South America* in 1846. Together, these volumes demonstrated Darwin's belief in Charles Lyell's theory, outlined in his *Principles of Geology*, that geological change took place gradually over vast periods of time. This idea of gradual change over time lay at the heart of Darwin's thinking as he returned to a field of scientific investigation closer to home. In 1846, intrigued by a specimen he had brought back from Chile and spurred on by his friend Joseph Hooker, Darwin began to classify all the known species, living and extinct, of Cirripedia, or barnacles.

Hooker was one of a coterie of friends and colleagues with whom Darwin corresponded, writing letters back and forth to, among others, the zoologist Thomas Henry Huxley, the geologist Adam Sedgwick and the influential Lyell, whom Darwin had met and befriended a decade earlier. Immersed in his routine of study, regular naps and circuits of the Sandwalk, Darwin found it easier to keep up his communications with the scientific community by post rather than tackle the journey into London by carriage and train. As he wrote to Captain FitzRoy in 1843, 'The little excitement of

Right: *Daguerreotype portrait of the Darwins' daughter Annie in 1849, aged eight. Annie died in 1851 at Malvern, Worcestershire, where her father had taken her in the hope of a cure. A week after her death, Darwin wrote down his memories of her, noting that 'the daguerreotype is very like her', but did not capture 'her dear face bright all the time, with the sweetest smiles'*
Below: *'Annie's box', her writing case housing an assortment of items collected by Emma in remembrance of her eldest daughter, and discovered in recent years by descendants. The box includes letters in Annie's looping handwriting, steel nibs and sealing wax, and a length of cream ribbon stitched with tiny glass beads*

breaking out of my routine so generally knocks me up, that I am able to do scarcely anything in London.'

The early years at Down were busy for Emma, too. From 1843 to 1856 she gave birth to seven more children: Henrietta 'Etty' (1843), George (1845), and Elizabeth 'Bessy' (1847) were followed by three more boys, Francis 'Frank' (1848), Leonard (1850), and Horace (1851). Emma was 48 when she had her last child, Charles Waring, in 1856. The household at Down also grew when, in 1848, Emma took on 19-year-old Catherine Thorley as a governess. Miss Thorley became part of the family, loved by Annie and dismissed as 'dull but worthy' by sharp-witted Etty.

It was characteristic of Darwin to bring the family into his working life outside the confines of the Old Study. For a number of summers during the early 1850s the children could be found racing across the lawns, shouting 'Here's a bee' from outposts around the garden, as part of a scheme to map the insects' flight paths. It was through the enforced break of a holiday away from Down, however, that the children saw their father at his most convivial. Etty recalled that when he was released from his work 'he entered into daily life with a youthfulness of enjoyment which made us feel we saw more of him in a week of holiday than in a month at home'.

In March 1849 the family decamped to Malvern in Worcestershire for three months, in pursuit of a remedy for Darwin's continued and debilitating ill health. Darwin received a water cure under the instruction of Dr James Manby Gully and there was a noticeable improvement in his symptoms, albeit a temporary one. When the family returned to Down in June, Darwin kept up the regime of cold bathing and scrubbing, logging his daily condition into a loose-leaf folio headed 'Diary of Health' which he kept for five years, and which shows that sickness and sleepless nights returned to plague him.

THE DEATH OF ANNIE

In 1850 the Darwins' eldest daughter, Annie, began to complain of headaches and feverishness. She grew worse as the months wore on, and Darwin took her to Malvern for treatment where she died shortly after Easter in 1851, probably from tuberculosis. Heavily pregnant with Horace, Emma had remained at Down, and Darwin returned at once to be with her, so Fanny Wedgwood attended the funeral at Malvern. Afterwards she wrote: 'I think everything was rightly arranged as you would have wished … there never could have been a child laid in the ground with truer sorrow round her than your sweet and happy Annie'. At Down, Emma put some of Annie's treasured possessions in her small writing case to remember her by: needlework, letters, trinkets and a lock of her hair bound in paper and dated the day of her death, 23 April 1851. This poignant memorial to a much-loved daughter was stored away for years and rediscovered by family descendants only recently. It is with the kind permission of the

Above: *Fancy Pigeons by J C Lyell. Darwin's copy is on the shelves in the Old Study*
Left: *Engraving illustrating the range of plumage that can be achieved by cross-breeding, an activity that fascinated Darwin. In the centre, a pouter exhibits its enormous 'crop', one of the most extreme variations*
Below: *The skeleton of a pigeon, annotated in Darwin's hand*

Keynes family that 'Annie's Box' is now on display at Down on the first floor.

The loss of his beloved Annie was for Darwin a 'bitter and cruel blow' from which he never truly recovered. He continued with his work on barnacles but with little enthusiasm, finally publishing the results of his classification work in two illustrated monographs in 1851 and 1854.

DARWIN THE PIGEON-FANCIER

In 1855 Darwin entered the arcane and not always salubrious world of the pigeon-fancier, where prime specimens were bred in pursuit of exotically plumed 'fancy' variants. He wanted to establish the common descent of all varieties of fancy pigeon from the wild African rock dove in order to show how their widely differing bodily forms, plumage and colouring have been developed by selective breeding. To this end, he constructed a pigeon house just beyond the service yard, enlisting 12-year-old Etty to help him look after a large collection of pouters, fantails and other pigeons.

Darwin mastered the art of dissecting birds at an early stage of development, boiling up the birds for their skeletons until the work became so repugnant that he farmed out the task to specialists. He joined London pigeon clubs – the exclusive Philoperisteron in Piccadilly, as well as another that met in a 'gin palace in Borough' where breeders gathered to swap birds and breeding tips. Darwin recognized that just as pigeon breeders drew out variations by breeding from the best specimens, so nature discarded the weak and allowed dominant variants to persist, giving him his opening argument for his theory of evolution by natural selection.

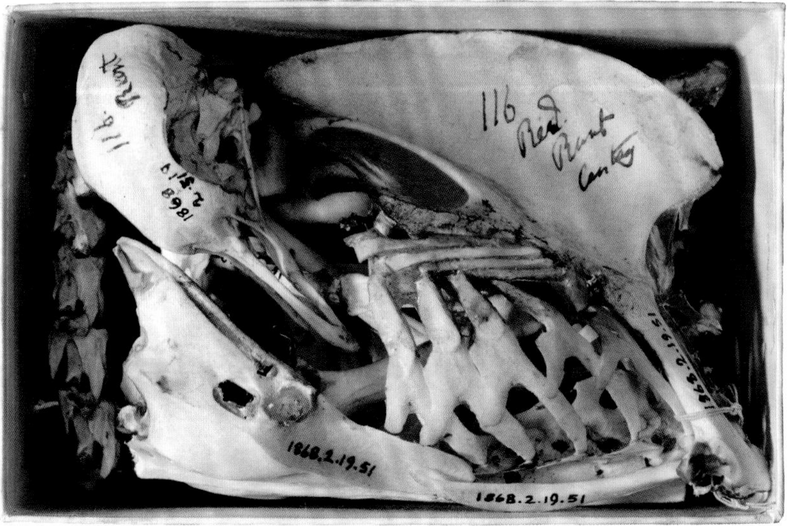

The Development of Down House

'As one of the bricklayers often says to me with a gloomy shake of his head, "A most deceptious property to buy, Sir"'

Charles Darwin to Susan Darwin, 27 April 1843

Down House was built in the early 18th century, probably on the site of a 17th-century house. It faced east and was a simple box shape (1).

In the late 18th century the house underwent a major modernization, probably soon after George Butler, a rich businessman and landowner, bought it in 1778. He built a new kitchen and service block onto the south end and rearranged and improved the principal rooms on the ground floor, moving the main entrance to the north side of the house and the staircase to its present position (2).

The house seems to have changed hands several times after Butler's death in 1783. Nathaniel Godbold, a property speculator from Fulham, acquired it in 1818 and rented it out to John Johnson, colonel of engineers in the Honourable East India Company, who later bought it. Johnson's son, William Arthur, sketched the house in about 1835, before the family moved to Canada. His two drawings are the only surviving pictures of the house as it was before the Darwins moved in (see illustration above). William later wrote a poem about his sister Catherine reminiscing on the shores of Lake Erie about her childhood home: 'She thought of the home where in youth she had played/Of the old house at 'Down', she remembered so well/Of the calm shady walks which at evening she strayed/Of the cowslip, the primrose and modest bluebell.'

The Revd J Drummond, vicar of Down, bought the house in 1837. He commissioned the architect and civil engineer Edward Cresy (1792–1858) to make some improvements, installing a new roof, two bathrooms, a stableyard and a cottage (3). Cresy lived locally and had recently surveyed and partially restored the nearby Eynsford Castle.

After the Darwins moved to Down in 1842 they employed Cresy to make further changes to the house. It is likely that he was responsible for the addition of a semi-octagonal three-window bay to the drawing room, which involved raising the ceiling and the height of the rooms above it.

From the first, Darwin found 'the publicity of the place intolerable', considering that the house stood 'very badly close to a tiny land & near another man's field.' He commissioned a builder to lower the lane that passed by the house and to lay out a new approach. Instead of having the entrance door facing north, as shown in W A Johnson's sketch, he built an external corridor along the north side of the house with the front door opening eastwards (4). He also built a wall, 6ft 6in (1.98m) high, the length of the property.

To accommodate his growing family, and appease his servants who complained about the inconvenient layout of the service block, in 1846 Darwin commissioned Cresy to build a new service wing. This provided extra offices and accommodation for the staff, both on the ground floor and in the roof space, and a schoolroom and extra bedroom on the first floor (5). There is no evidence to suggest that Darwin engaged Cresy after this but the two saw each other socially, and Darwin corresponded with Cresy's son Edward on scientific subjects and helped to secure him a job at the Metropolitan Board of Works.

In 1857 the Darwins decided that their dining room was not large enough to accommodate themselves and all their cousins when they came to stay, and so they commissioned a new one with a large bedroom over it. Finished in 1858, this two-storey extension was built on the north end of the house and projected slightly into the garden (6). On completion, however, the Darwins decided to use the light and airy ground-floor room, with French doors opening on to the lawn, as a drawing room. In 1872 they added a verandah.

Apart from minor alterations, no further changes were made to the house until 1876, when the architect William Cecil Marshall was engaged to build an extension on the north side of the house. This was originally intended as a billiard room with adjacent corridor and rooms above (7), and was probably instigated by the arrival of the Darwins' son Francis, who came to live at Down with his baby son, Bernard, that same year. Darwin then turned this room into his New Study.

Darwin also made numerous changes to the grounds around Down House. The laboratory, built in 1881, was built as a darkroom with fittings for experiments on plant growth towards light, although he never used it.

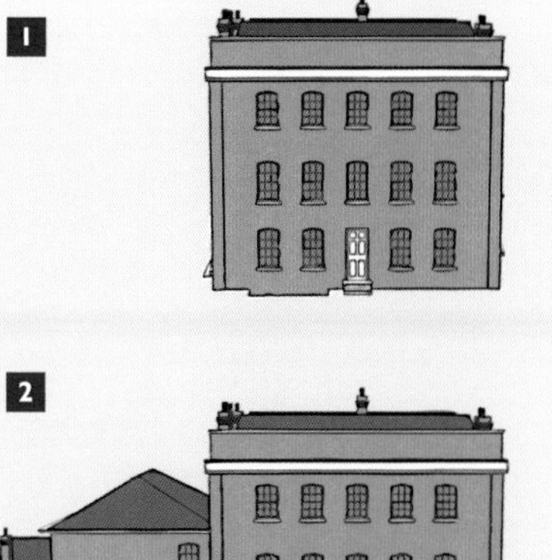

1 *The original Georgian house in about 1730–40*

2 *In the late 1770s, a kitchen wing is added and the front door is moved to the side*

3 *In about 1837, the architect Edward Cresy adds a new roof, and the house is rendered*

4 *In 1843, not long after their arrival, the Darwins begin to make changes, moving the front door and adding a full-height projecting bay on the west side of the house*

5 *In about 1846, the Darwins expand the kitchen wing, adding offices on the ground floor and a schoolroom and bedrooms upstairs*

6 *In 1858, they add a new drawing room with bedroom above*

7 *In 1876, a two-storey extension is added. The new ground-floor room becomes Darwin's New Study*

Facing page: View of Down House from the north, by W A Johnson, about 1835. This sketch is the earliest known depiction of Down House, drawn before the arrival of the Darwins. It shows the house with its original roof. One of Darwin's first actions on moving here was to have the lane lowered to prevent passers-by being able to peer in

***Right:** Portrait of Alfred Russel Wallace painted in the 1950s by Russian artist Evstafieff. Wallace spent many years travelling in South-East Asia, and it was from Malaysia that he mailed his momentous letter to Darwin, outlining his similar theory, in June 1858*

PUBLICATION OF *ON THE ORIGIN OF SPECIES*, 1855–9

In October 1844 Darwin wrote to the Revd Leonard Jenyns, an old beetling companion from his Cambridge days, admitting that, 'The general conclusion at which I have slowly been driven from a directly opposite conviction is that species are mutable & that allied species are co-descendants of common stocks. I know how much I open myself, to reproach, for such a conclusion but I have at least honestly & deliberately come to it'.

Darwin's letter makes clear that in 1844, at the time of the first draft of his 'species theory', he understood the enormous significance of his conclusion. A few months before he began writing his 1844 essay he had written to Joseph Hooker to disclose his conviction that 'species are not (it is like confessing a murder) immutable' and that he understood implicitly the importance of preparing the ground thoroughly to 'give all arguments & facts on both sides' when the time came.

Ten years later, Darwin's work on barnacles gave him the credibility to speak as a scientific authority, with a body of published research to his name. From his study and gardens at Down House he now pursued several lines of enquiry to further cement his theory. In 1855, parallel to his pigeon-breeding activities, Darwin began a series of experiments to test seed survival. He wanted to demonstrate that it was possible for seeds to survive a long and variable journey from one land mass to another where they might germinate and produce a new species in geographical isolation from the point of origin.

Among these dispersal experiments Darwin soaked varieties of seeds in dozens of bottles of salt water, recovering the seeds at intervals and keeping them in dishes crowded on his mantelpiece in the Old Study, where he watched over them. He delighted in new sproutings, using the *Gardeners' Chronicle* to publish short notices on successful outcomes, notably his discovery that seeds could germinate after more than a month 'at sea'.

From 1856 onwards Darwin began to write up his theory. He did not find it easy and, according to Henrietta, was 'apt to invert his sentences both in writing and speaking, putting the qualifying clause before you knew what it was to qualify'. By June 1858, however, he was more than two-thirds of the way through when he received a startling letter from a young naturalist, Alfred Russel Wallace, with whom he had corresponded during his research. It contained a summary of Wallace's theory of natural selection, with conclusions identical to Darwin's own. Darwin turned to Lyell for advice, who proposed that Darwin and Wallace should prepare a joint announcement to the scientific community. As Darwin's youngest son was mortally ill with scarlet fever, Lyell enlisted Hooker's help and, on 1 July 1858, together they presented a joint paper to the Linnean Society that brought together Wallace's abstract with extracts from Darwin's crucial 1844 species essay. The paper was published in the Linnean Society journal that year as *On the tendency of species to form varieties; and on the perpetuation of varieties and species by means of selection*, but, surprisingly, neither the public reading nor the published paper raised even a murmur of interest. At least Wallace, 'admirably free from envy or jealousy', had been content to remain in Darwin's shadow.

The year was full of upheaval at Down. Darwin's youngest son, Charles Waring, died at

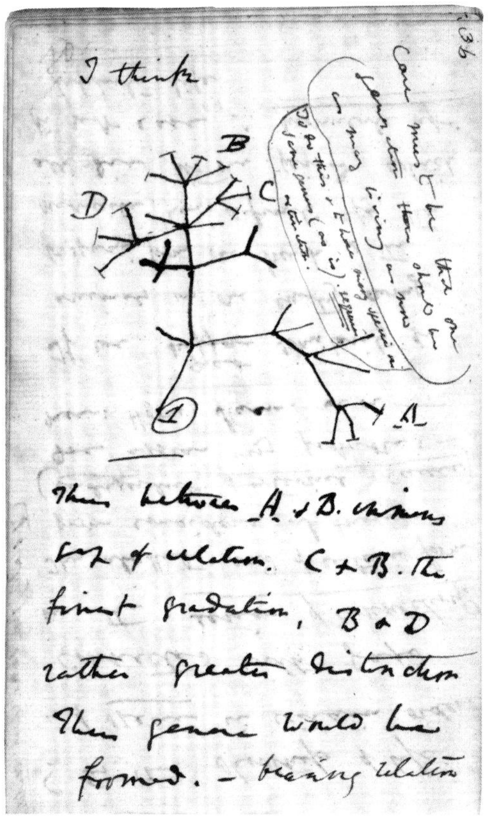

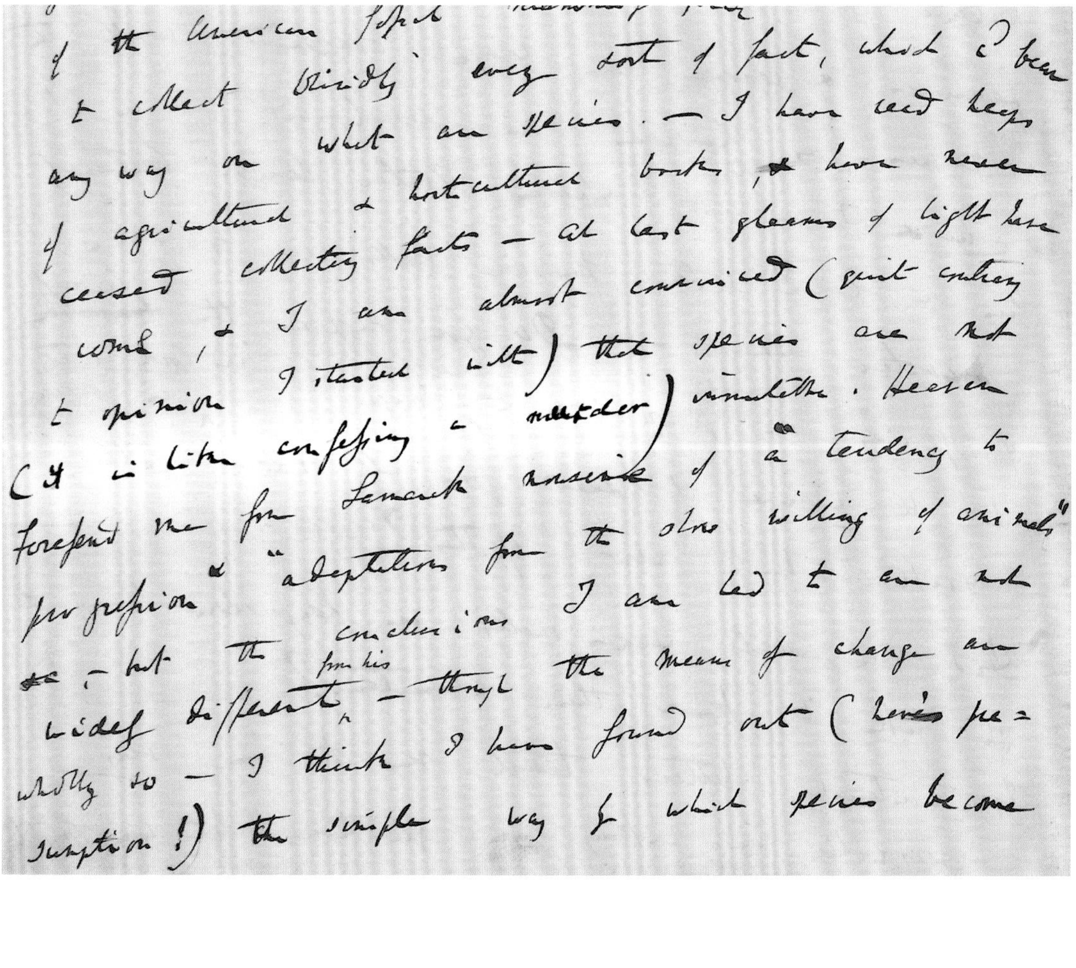
of the American ... to collect blindly every sort of fact, which could bear any way on what are species. — I have read heaps of agricultural & horticultural books, & have never ceased collecting facts — at last gleams of light have come, & I am almost convinced (quite contrary to opinion I started with) that species are not (it is like confessing a murder) immutable. Heaven forfend me from Lamarck nonsense of a "tendency to progression" "adaptations from the slow willing of animals" &c, — but the conclusions I am led to are not widely different from his — though the means of change are wholly so — I think I have found out (here's presumption!) the simple way by which species become

Left: *In 1837 Darwin sketched out this first branch diagram to explain the process of evolution as he saw it, introduced with the tentative words, 'I think'. The base of the diagram marks the point of origin, with those branches leading to further variations marked with lines at the tip; those branches without lines indicate extinction. Darwin developed this diagram significantly before publishing a more elaborate version in* On the Origin of Species

Below: *Letter from Charles Darwin to Joseph Hooker, dated 11 January 1844, in which Darwin claims that admitting species are not immutable 'is like confessing a murder' (see highlighted area)*

Right: *In 1925, the controversy over Darwin's theory of evolution came to a head in the USA, when John T Scopes was put on trial in Dayton, Tennessee, for teaching evolution in schools. Here, anti-evolutionists sell books in defence of their beliefs*
Below: *This present-day American bumper sticker, showing a dinosaur devouring the Christian symbol of a fish, symbolizes the ongoing debate between the evolutionists and the creationists*

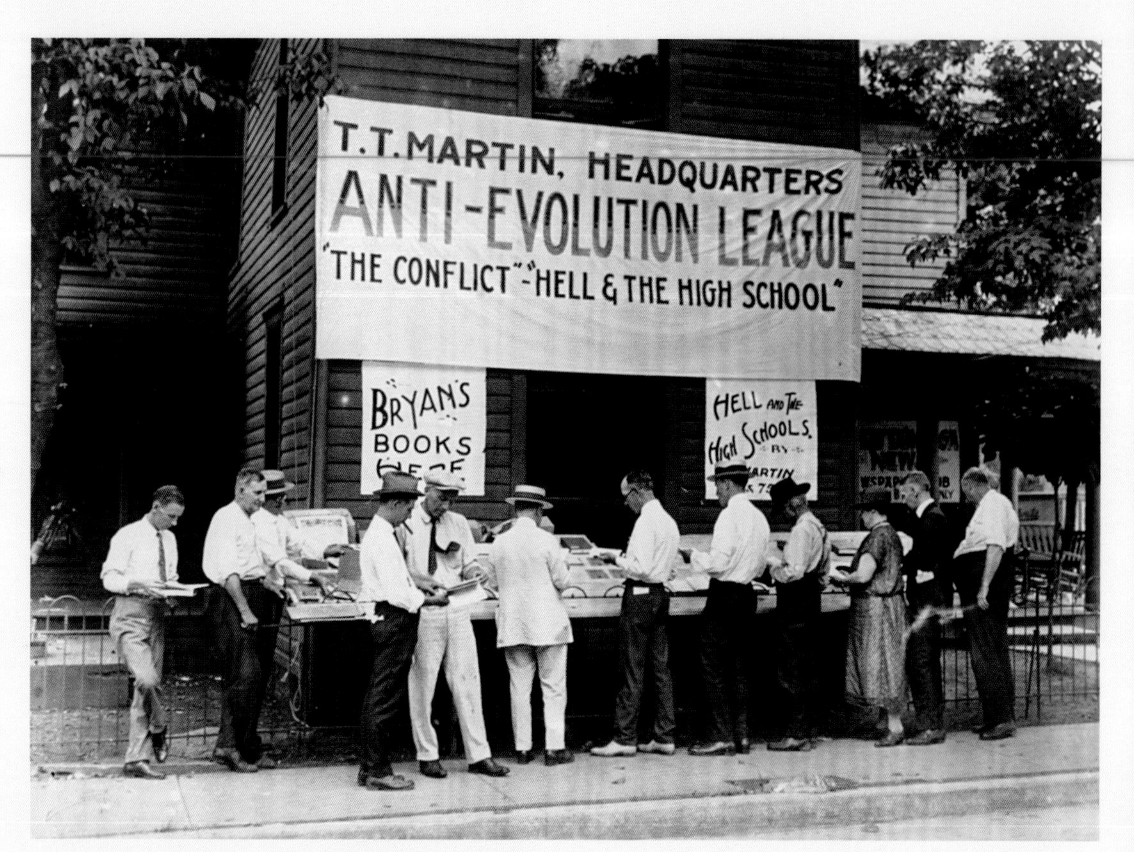

'Evolutionism is a fairy tale for grown-ups. This theory has helped nothing in the progress of science. It is useless'
Louis Bounoure, professor of biology at Strasbourg University, writing in The Advocate, *8 March 1984*

Darwin's Legacy

At the time of Darwin's death, *On the Origin of Species* was in its sixth edition and, together with his other works, was known throughout the world in dozens of translations from Chinese to Romanian. During his lifetime Darwin's ideas were promulgated as 'Darwinism', a phrase coined by Thomas Henry Huxley and supported in numerous works espousing his theory of evolution by natural selection. After Darwin's death, a rash of books was published which used 'Darwinism' to support many philosophical ideas dependent on evolutionary theory.

In the late 19th century the term 'social Darwinism' was used to mean social evolution through human competition, or 'survival of the fittest'. The term became popular in the early 20th century in the light of eugenics – a word created by Darwin's cousin, Francis Galton, to mean intervention, such as controlled breeding, to improve the human stock. The use of eugenics by Nazi and other fascist political regimes to justify mass extermination meant that advocates of Darwin have had to fight to reclaim the original theory from far more sinister interpretations.

During the late 20th century many publications in the field of social science examined Darwin's life and work. A new edition of his *Beagle* diary was also published (in 1988), along with transcriptions of his notebooks and new biographies, notably *Darwin* by Adrian Desmond and James Moore (1991). The Darwin Correspondence Project, based at the University Library in Cambridge, is tackling his correspondence, publishing (in 1985) the first of a projected 32-volume series, which will bring every aspect of Darwin's life and work into focus for the 21st century.

As histories and interpretations of his life and work continue to be written, Darwin's theory of evolution remains under constant scrutiny. Creationism and, in recent years, the emergence of the concept of 'intelligent design' as an alternative explanation for the development of species (according to which evolution is driven by divine intelligence rather than natural selection) shows that the implications of evolutionary theory for human origins – so contentious for Darwin in his lifetime – remain as controversial today.

the end of June, and the house was filled with the noise and dust of extension works. Darwin took his family to the Isle of Wight to recuperate, where, in response to Hooker's urging that he reach a swift conclusion following Wallace's abstract, he started work on a summary version of his theory of evolution. He finally laid down his pen at Down in April 1859, having written 155,000 words. The finished manuscript differed from his original plan for a three-volume work aimed at the scientific reader and contained a minimum number of references and illustrations.

Darwin had been led to his theory of natural selection through reflection on his observations of natural life. From his days on the *Beagle* he had noticed minor differences between individuals of the same species, and his detailed examination of the various barnacle species had confirmed this. Through detailed research he established that specimens better fitted to survive in their surroundings had a greater chance of survival, and that sexual reproduction sustained modifications present in the better adapted specimens. He also observed that all species produce more offspring than can survive on the resources to hand. This produces a struggle in which those best able to survive do so.

On the Origin of Species linked all these points together to provide an explanation for the 'preservation of favoured races in the struggle for life' that appealed to the scientist and 'common reader' alike. Confident in the recommendation of Lyell, the renowned publisher John Murray agreed to publish Darwin's manuscript, unseen, with a print run of 500 copies. On 24 November 1859, after some refinement of the text and title, the work was published as *On the Origin of Species by Means of Natural Selection, or the Preservation of Favoured Races in the Struggle for Life*. Exhausted by the effort of production, Darwin retreated to Wells House spa on Ilkley Moor in Yorkshire where, 'living in Hell' with 'a rash and fiery Boils', and nothing but billiards to distract him, he awaited the verdict.

REACTION TO THE PUBLICATION

Dozens of complimentary copies of *On the Origin of Species* were posted to Darwin's peers in the scientific fraternity and an expanded print run of

Left: *Joseph Hooker, botanist and director of the Royal Botanic Gardens at Kew, was Darwin's lifelong ally, and defended Darwin's position vigorously in the face of public criticism of* On the Origin of Species. *This stern portrait is one of three pictures given a special place above the mantelpiece in Darwin's Old Study, hanging as it does alongside portraits of Charles Lyell and Josiah Wedgwood I*

Below: *The spine and title page of Darwin's* On the Origin of Species, *published by John Murray on 24 November 1859*

ON

THE ORIGIN OF SPECIES

BY MEANS OF NATURAL SELECTION,

OR THE

PRESERVATION OF FAVOURED RACES IN THE STRUGGLE FOR LIFE.

BY CHARLES DARWIN, M.A.,

FELLOW OF THE ROYAL, GEOLOGICAL, LINNÆAN, ETC., SOCIETIES; AUTHOR OF 'JOURNAL OF RESEARCHES DURING H. M. S. BEAGLE'S VOYAGE ROUND THE WORLD.'

LONDON:
JOHN MURRAY, ALBEMARLE STREET.
Nov. 24 1859.

The right of Translation is reserved.

Right: *The biologist Thomas Henry Huxley with a sketch of a gorilla skull, about 1870. Huxley's vehement defence of Darwin's theory of evolution led him to be known as 'Darwin's bulldog'. He wrote a number of positive reviews of* On the Origin of Species *in the months after its publication, and clashed publicly with the foremost critic of the theory, the bishop of Oxford, Samuel Wilberforce*

Below right: *Darwin shares his likeness with an ape in a cartoon from the* London Sketchbook *of 1874. Many cartoonists of the day played on the idea of a physical resemblance between the hirsute Darwin and an ape*

Below: *The bishop of Oxford, Samuel Wilberforce, nicknamed Soapy Sam because of his claim, 'I am often in hot water, and always come out with clean hands'. He famously challenged Darwin's theory at a debate in Oxford in June 1860*

1,250 copies sold out immediately. While John Murray hastily reprinted, Darwin returned from Yorkshire to Down House, where he prepared a second edition of the book. Supportive reviews began to appear in publications from *The Times* to the *Gardeners' Chronicle*, but it was Richard Owen, writing a scathing piece for the *Edinburgh Review* in April 1860, who landed the first blow. Owen was a renowned anatomist and palaeontologist, and sometime correspondent of Darwin, who had worked on the fossil volume of *The Zoology of the Voyage of HMS Beagle*. The two had been colleagues and Darwin was aggrieved by what he viewed as Owen's wilful misinterpretation of his theory, most likely on grounds of his intense dislike of Darwin's ally, Thomas Henry Huxley.

Jealous critics aside, Darwin's book posed genuinely problematic questions for 19th-century society. Although scientists could accept the idea of a process of evolution, there was difficulty in accepting that this could have happened without reference to an all-powerful creator. Although Darwin had been keen to avoid 'man' in his work, the conclusion was there to be drawn that, as Huxley said, 'man might be a transmuted ape'.

THE OXFORD DEBATE

Given the rigorous research underpinning his theory, Darwin could answer 'all arguments and facts on both sides', but he chose to remain at Down House as the debate took hold, preferring his allies to lead the charge. It says much about Darwin's support network that he could rely on such staunch support from his friends. Huxley's public rebuttals in published articles of Owen's caustic review laid the ground for a debate held by the British Association for the Advancement of Science in Oxford, in June 1860.

The bishop of Oxford, Samuel Wilberforce (1805–73), a brilliant public speaker, raised a sneering challenge to 'civilisation according to the Darwinian hypothesis'. As vice-president of the British Association of the Advancement of Science, Wilberforce was certainly entitled to challenge Darwin on a scientific subject, but on this occasion he was roundly silenced by the counter arguments from Huxley and Hooker.

Left: *Darwin photographed in 1867, astride his horse Tommy at the entrance to Down House. He took up riding as a form of exercise on the recommendation of his doctor. 'He used to say it prevented him from thinking much more effectually than walking,' Etty recalled. 'He liked the friendly recognition he met with … there was always a great deal of curtseying & grinning of the children in the village.' In 1869, however, Darwin suffered a bad fall while out riding on Keston Common and took to a sturdier mare, before giving up altogether a year or two later*

LIFE AFTER THE *ORIGIN*

Darwin had turned 50, and Emma 51, in the year in which *On the Origin of Species* was finally published after a gestation period of nearly 20 years. In that time they had created a life at Down House that suited them perfectly, developing the bare bones of the 'ugly' house and grounds into a retreat from the outside world. The earliest known photograph of Down House dates from 1860 and shows the view from the garden, the dining-room bay with trellis, and three figures in the middle-distance. By this time, the house had been transformed, with comfortable rooms, if rather shabby through use, spreading out from the original square block, and views across the garden and the meadows beyond. The kitchen garden and the orchard provided fruit and vegetables which, together with livestock including chickens, cows and pigs, allowed the Darwins to live a self-sufficient life with little recourse to the world beyond Downe.

In 1860 the Darwin's seven surviving children were aged from nine to 21. The eldest, William, was following in his father's footsteps at Christ's College, Cambridge, the two middle boys, Francis and George, were boarders at Clapham School in south London, while the two youngest boys, Leonard and Horace, lived at home with their sisters Henrietta and Elizabeth. Visitors dropped in and out of a family life that, for Darwin, trod the well-worn path of established routine: work in the Old Study, punctuated with lunch at one o'clock, regular perambulations around the Sandwalk and an evening game of backgammon with Emma.

Darwin's letter-writing commitments had increased to burdensome levels as *On the Origin of Species* spread his reputation. 'No doubt the public has been shamefully imposed on! For they bought the book, thinking that it would be nice easy reading', he wrote to Asa Gray on hearing that copies of the *Origin* were on sale at Waterloo station. Gray, an American naturalist and long-time friend, was instrumental in extracting a good deal from a New York publisher for the book's first American edition, published in 1860.

Hunched at his chair and writing board in the Old Study, Darwin's thoughts took him beyond new editions of the book. In his haste to publish, the version that had emerged only partly covered the breadth of his work under the umbrella

Right: *Illustrations from* The Expression of the Emotions in Man and Animals, *published in 1872. Darwin's last major work, this was one of the first books to employ photographs as illustrations*

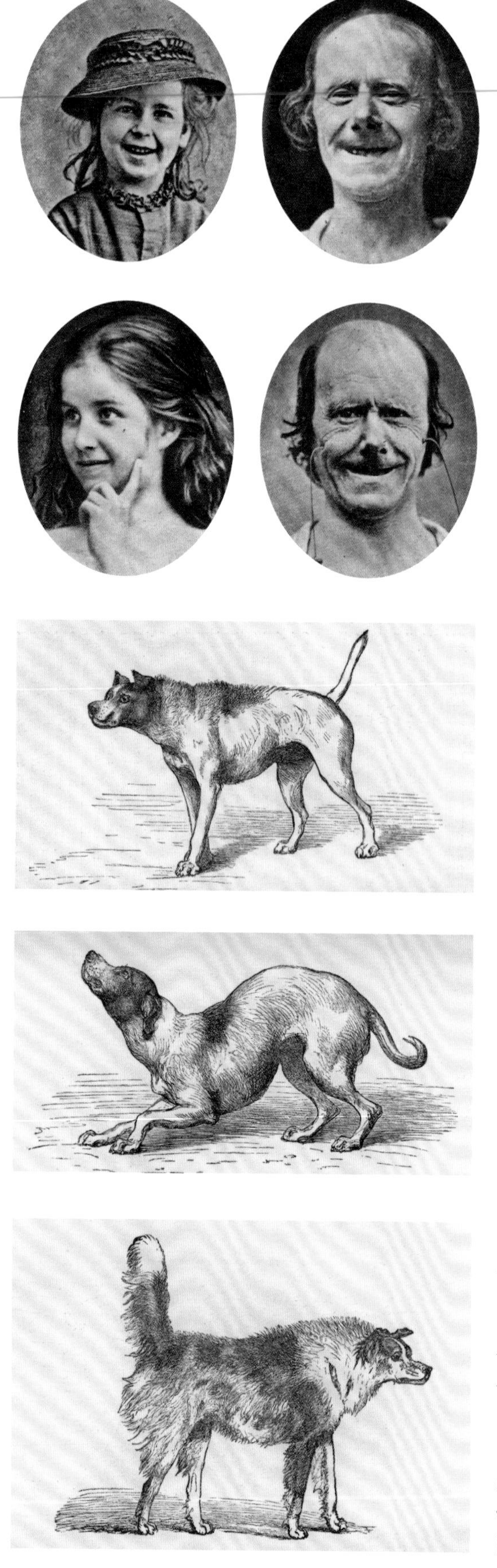

of 'natural selection'. During the 1860s Darwin expanded his thoughts on variation, pulling together unpublished chapters and various strands of research on birds and plant species. In 1868 he published *The Variation of Animals and Plants under Domestication* in two volumes, which included for the first time the phrase 'survival of the fittest', coined by Herbert Spencer in preference to 'natural selection'.

As ever, Darwin was slowed in his work by his perpetual ill health. He suffered particularly bad episodes in 1861 and 1865, and was confined to his bed, compelled to dictate letters to Emma as he lay enfeebled by the recurrent onslaught of vomiting, flatulence and severe headaches. He put himself in the hands of successive doctors and treatments but relief was always short-lived and the symptoms returned. In 1862, scaly with eczema and hollow-cheeked from an attempt to settle his stomach by restrictive diet, Darwin grew a full beard. This transformed his appearance to such an extent that on a rare visit to London acquaintances faltered before recognizing him.

Several photographic portraits of Darwin were made during the 1860s, most notably one by the pioneering photographer Julia Margaret Cameron, whom Darwin had met while convalescing on the Isle of Wight in 1868. Her portrait of Darwin at the age of 59 now hangs in the billiard room.

When his illness abated, Darwin worked on the botanical experiments in the gardens and greenhouse at Down that characterized his working life post-*Origin*. These investigations prompted a second tier of publications, the first of which was *On the Various Contrivances by which British and Foreign Orchids are Fertilised by Insects* (1862). In this work Darwin demonstrated how intricate variations in the design of different orchids evolved to assist insect cross-pollination. A paper for the Linnean Society finally published in 1875 as *The Movement and Habits of Climbing Plants* was the result of observations on more than 100 climbing-plant species and their reactions to light and other stimuli (see pages 20–25 for Darwin's garden and greenhouse experiments).

Meanwhile, *The Descent of Man, and Selection in Relation to Sex* was published as a two-volume work in 1871. It confronted the subject of human evolution head-on, establishing an evolutionary family tree from monkey to man, and suggesting that human morality had simply evolved from our social instincts. Its publication was greeted with large sales and a slew of caricatures and cartoons in the national press. The following year Darwin tackled the development and physiognomy of human and animal expressions in *The Expression of the Emotions in Man and Animals*.

In completing this volume Darwin finished the corpus of work on evolution and human descent that had begun with *On the Origin of Species*, the product of more than 30 years of thought and experimentation, and almost all of it undertaken at Down House. The house had certainly repaid the initial investment of £2,000, more than doubling in size during this period. In 1876, a final campaign of building work saw a two-storey wing tacked on to the north corner of the house, providing a bedroom and drawing room for the Darwins' recently-returned son Francis (see page 13) on the first floor and a proposed new billiard room beneath, an arrangement that allowed Francis the use of the old billiard room as a study, alongside his father's. In 1872, Darwin had added a glass-roofed verandah with an encaustic tiled floor on to the drawing room. Here he enjoyed his last summers, sitting in the comfort of his wicker chair, overlooking a Kentish garden in bloom and the meadows beyond.

Above: *Photograph of Charles Darwin sitting on the verandah at Down House in the late 1870s*
Left: *Watercolour by Julia 'Snow' Wedgwood, showing the flowerbeds and climbers at Down House in full bloom*

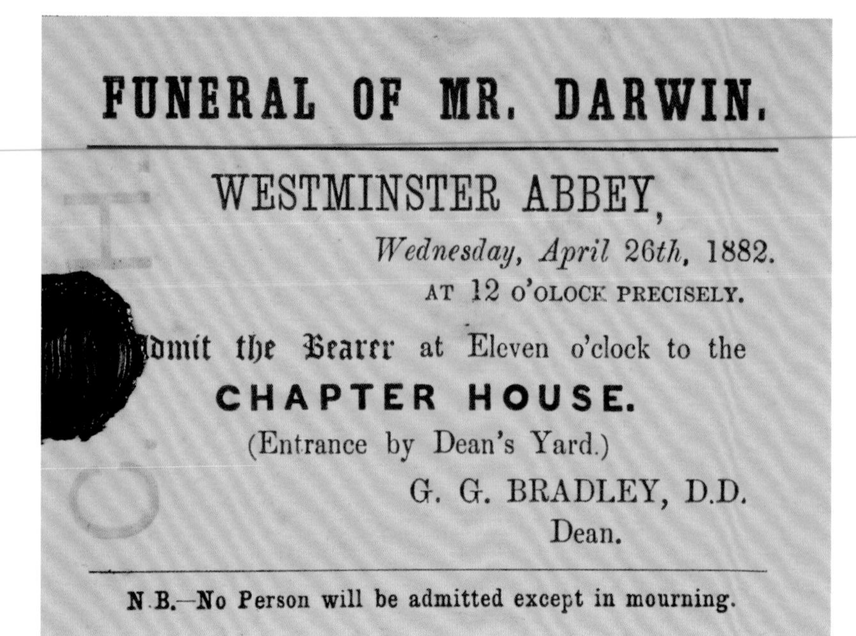

FUNERAL OF MR. DARWIN.

WESTMINSTER ABBEY,

Wednesday, April 26th, 1882.

AT 12 O'CLOCK PRECISELY.

Admit the Bearer at Eleven o'clock to the

CHAPTER HOUSE.

(Entrance by Dean's Yard.)

G. G. BRADLEY, D.D.

Dean.

N.B.—No Person will be admitted except in mourning.

Above: *Entry card to Charles Darwin's funeral at Westminster Abbey. Darwin was interred close to the monument to Sir Isaac Newton, at the north end of the choir screen*

Right: *Darwin's funeral at Westminster Abbey, where the most distinguished members of Victorian society gathered to pay their last respects to one of the age's most influential figures, illustrated in* The Graphic, *1882*

DARWIN'S FINAL YEARS

In 1843, soon after moving into his new home, Darwin had written, 'My life goes on as clockwork, I am fixed in the place where I shall end it'. Almost 40 years on, at the beginning of the 1880s, Darwin felt his life drawing to a close at Down House. While Emma remained fit at 72, the burdens of old age and years of ill-health were beginning to take their toll on 71-year-old Darwin, and work became increasingly onerous to him. The biggest change in his life during his final years was the move from the Old Study to the New Study at the north end of the house (now the ticket office and shop). A creature of habit, Darwin recreated the proportions of his old study with a bookcase running along the west wall, thereby closing off the door to the garden, and positioned his furniture and the various pictures above the mantelpiece in the same fashion, the effect captured in a contemporary photograph from this period (see page 5).

In early April 1882 Darwin suffered an attack of angina on the Sandwalk, and on 19 April he died with Emma and the children at his bedside. Huxley and Lubbock petitioned the House of Commons to allow the great scientist a fitting burial and newspapers ran patriotic notices. 'Darwin died, as he had lived, in the quiet retirement of the country home which he had loved', *The Standard* eulogized, amid 'the simple plants and animals that enabled him to solve the great enigma of the Origin of Species'. After some deliberation the family consented to his burial at Westminster Abbey and on 26 April he was interred there 'among the illustrious dead' in a ceremony attended by the most distinguished members of Victorian society.

Left: Watercolour of Down House in the early 20th century when it was home to Downe House School, painted by Dorothy Willis, sister of the school's founder, Olive Willis

Below: Pupils and staff of Downe House School in 1909, photographed on the back lawn in front of the dining room window. The proprietor and headmistress Miss Olive Willis is in the middle of the second row

DOWN HOUSE AFTER THE DARWINS

After Darwin's death, Emma, together with the children and grandchildren still resident at Down House, moved to Cambridge, a favoured place from Francis Darwin's university days, although Emma returned every year to spend her summers at Down until her death in 1896. The children kept the house on, unoccupied, until the turn of the century, at which point there followed a succession of short-term tenancies.

In 1907 the house became Downe School for Girls (later Downe House School), run successfully under the governance of Miss Olive Willis until 1921, when the school moved to larger premises in Cold Ash, Berkshire. Another school opened in its place but failed to emulate Miss Willis's success, and Down House languished empty for a few years, in an increasing state of disrepair.

The master of Darwin's alma mater, Christ's College, Cambridge, brought the plight of the house to the attention of Sir Arthur Keith, curator of the Hunterian Museum at the Royal College of Surgeons. Sir Arthur used his 1927 presidential address to the British Association for the Advancement of Science (BAAS) to make a plea for support to preserve Down House as a national memorial to Darwin, and found a benefactor for the cause in an eminent surgeon, Sir George Buckston Browne. Sir George was able to buy Down House for £4,250 and foot a further bill of £10,000 for repairs to the house and to remove outbuildings added by Miss Willis during the school's tenure. In the space of two years Down House was restored, with the help of Darwin's only surviving son Leonard, who used his photographs and memories of Down House in his father's lifetime to recreate Darwin's Old Study, and the family returned many pictures and other possessions that remain at the house to this day.

Above: *Thirteen of Darwin's great-grandchildren gather for a family photograph in the grounds of Down House, to celebrate its opening as a museum, 7 June 1929*

With a generous endowment of £2,000 from Sir George, Down House was opened to the public as a museum on 7 June 1929, under the care of the BAAS. A series of photographs marking the occasion shows guests thronging the lawn in front of the revived rear façade of the house, a testimony to Sir George's generosity and commitment.

Apart from a period of closure during the Second World War, the 'Darwin Museum' was maintained by the BAAS, and then by the Royal College of Surgeons, for nearly 60 years. Day-to-day care of the house fell to a succession of resident honorary curators. Dr O J R Howarth, the first curator, lived with his wife Eleanor in an apartment on the first and second floors of the house, with Sam Robinson as custodian of the house living at first in the adjacent cottage, and then in the servants' wing of the main house. Dr Howarth occupied Down House until his death in 1954, and Robinson until his death in 1958, when his son Sydney became custodian until his retirement in 1974.

Another key figure in the history of Down House as a museum was Sir Hedley Atkins, former President of the Royal College of Surgeons. Sir Hedley took a keen interest in the house in the 1970s, publishing a book entitled *Down: Home of the Darwins* (1974) and overseeing major repairs. Like his predecessor, Sir Hedley lived at Down House, with his wife Lady Gladwys, until his death in 1983.

In the late 1980s the Royal College of Surgeons ceded responsibility for Down House to the Natural History Museum, hoping that a permanent solution could be found for the management of a building again in need of repair. Finally, in 1996, the house passed into the care of English Heritage, which bought Down House and its contents with generous support from the Wellcome Trust and the Heritage Lottery Fund. English Heritage's first commitment was to undertake major structural repairs to ensure the long-term stability of Down House for public access. The arrangement of the rooms in Darwin's day was recreated on the ground-floor, and an exhibition exploring his life and work was installed on the first floor. The house reopened to visitors in 1998, and in that year a long-term programme of work was begun to restore the gardens.

Downe House School for Girls

One of the school's first pupils, Nan Napier, reminisces about happy days spent at Down House:

'Like all houses, Downe [sic] had its own character, gracious and light with a sense of space and great friendliness, the garden a child's paradise with wide lawns, trees to climb, and a wood to prowl in full of primroses in spring. There are memories of so many things which went to make those first terms full of happiness and fun. When I hear Bach's double violin concerto the picture in my mind is of the dining room at Downe, where [Hilary Willis and I] practised and played it together with such joy. There was the excitement of new developments … New classrooms were equipped, the playing field was made, the laboratory in the garden was opened and here Miss Heather presided over the bangs and smells. What an honour to be working in Darwin's own laboratory! Hilary always had the impression that he was perhaps quite close to us. In the evenings, round the drawing-room fire while we sewed and mended, Miss Willis read to us as no one else has ever read except perhaps her father. No picture of Downe is complete without the old mulberry tree on which mulberries grew really black and ripe and luscious and under which we sometimes had lessons. There were jaunts to the theatre, travelling in a double-decker bus with lively competition for the front seats on top. The country roads seemed to go to the London drivers' heads and the bus would career down the hills and round the corners. Coming home on snowy roads was an exciting adventure; on one foggy occasion we took it in turn to walk in front of the bus waving a handkerchief to guide the driver.'

'What an honour to be working in Darwin's own laboratory. Hilary always had the impression that he was perhaps quite close to us'

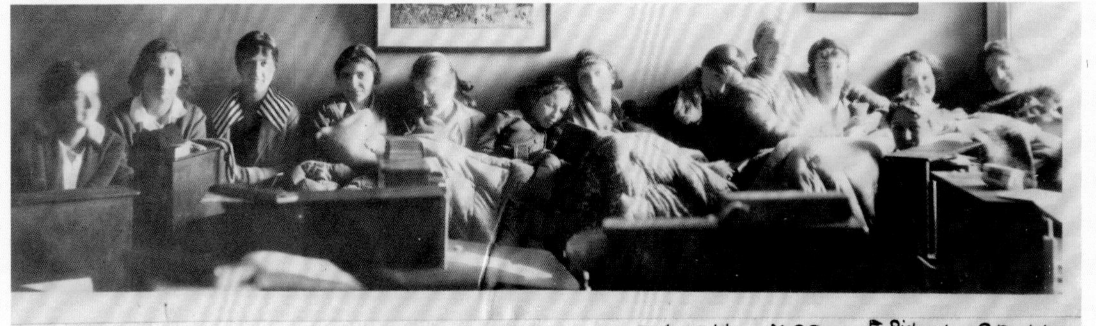

Crook. V. Newnham. K. Ranken. I. Butler. T. Sanders. F. Butler. B. Ruxton. J. Sly. F. Wills. M.P.B. E. Richards. C. Lawrance. P. Erskine.

"If we mayn't have hot pipes, we'll have to —

M. Crook. V. Newnham. K. Ranken. I. Butler. T. Sanders. F. Butler. B. Ruxton. J. Sly. F. Wills. M.P.B. E. Richard. C. Lawrance.

— keep ourselves warm by other means."

Above: *Nan Napier (née Woodall, 1895–1973), the first girl registered at Downe House School when it opened in 1907*

Left: *A pair of informal photographs showing pupils at Downe House School trying to keep warm, from an album given to Down House by Nan Napier*

DOWN HOUSE TODAY

Since reopening its doors to the public in April 1998, Down House has welcomed tens of thousands of visitors from across the globe. Interest in Darwin's life and work continues to grow; his groundbreaking theory is an accepted part of our understanding of the world around us and remains at the heart of scientific thought in the 21st century.

To celebrate the bicentenary of Darwin's birth in 2009, a new exhibition was designed to show the development of Darwin's scientific theories in the context of his life as a naturalist in the Victorian age. The gardens have been fully restored, and an interactive tour of the gardens highlights Darwin's key experiments, many of which have been recreated for visitors to see at first hand. In 2016, Charles and Emma Darwin's bedroom was also recreated, highlighting the fact that Down House, above all else, was a family home.

Right: *A reconstruction of Darwin's cabin on HMS* Beagle *can be found on the first floor. It is based on contemporary diagrams and sketches, one of which is annotated in Darwin's own hand, and contains Darwin's own books and scientific instruments*

Below: *The garden front of Down House, with a recreation of Darwin's lawn plot experiment (see page 20) in the foreground*